MGB GT V8

Driver's Handbook

Publication Part No. AKD 8423 (4th Edition)

Leyland Cars—Sales
Longbridge, Birmingham B31 2TB, England

Leyland Cars—Service
Cowley, Oxford OX4 2PG, England

This Handbook introduces you to your British Leyland car. Your car is built to a high standard of quality and reliability and with good driving, correct car care and regular maintenance should give you carefree and economical motoring.

The introductory pages cover the operation and function of the controls, switches and general equipment fitted.

The main part of the Handbook gives detailed information on jacking, wheel changing, bulb renewal, lubrication and the servicing procedure of components.

Regular maintenance at the recommended intervals is essential to maintain your car at the original standard of efficiency and you will find our detailed recommendations under 'ROUTINE MAINTENANCE SUMMARY'. Those items which require specialized equipment should be carried out by a Distributor or Dealer. Refer to the 'GENERAL DATA' for information required during servicing and the day-to-day running of the vehicle such as tyre pressures, oil capacities, etc.

Our Distributors and Dealers are trained and available to service your car for you, and details of our maintenance scheme are included in your **Passport to Service**. Look for the **Leycare** sign.

References to right- or left-hand are made as if the car is being viewed from the rear.

CONTENTS

CONTROLS Fig. 1

Gear lever (1)
The gear positions are indicated on the lever knob. To engage reverse gear move the lever to the left in the neutral position until resistance is felt, apply further side pressure to overcome the resistance and then pull the lever back to engage the gear. The reverse lights operate automatically when reverse is selected with the ignition switched on.

Synchromesh engagement is provided on all forward gears.

Hand brake (2)
The hand brake is of the pull-up lever type, operating mechanically on the rear wheels only. To release the hand brake, pull the lever up slightly, depress the button on the end of the lever and push the lever down.

Pedals (3) (4) (5)
The brake pedal operates the brake hydraulic system and applies the brakes on all four wheels. The brake stop warning lights function automatically when the brake pedal is depressed with the ignition switched on.

Mixture control (choke) (6)
Use the control to enrich the mixture and assist starting when the engine is cold. The fuel/air mixture is progressively enriched as the control is pulled out.

Pull out the control to the required position and lock it by turning the control clockwise one-quarter of a turn.

To re-position the control or return it to the 'OFF' position, turn the knob anti-clockwise one-quarter of a turn and push inwards.

DO NOT MOVE the control in or out whilst it is in the 'locked' position.

Notes on the use of the control are given in **'STARTING AND RUNNING IN-STRUCTIONS'.**

Fig. 1

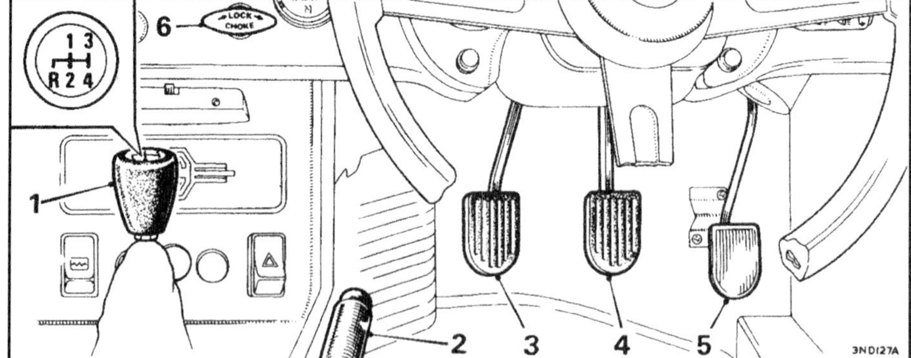

IGNITION STARTER SWITCH AND STEERING LOCK Fig. 2

Key number The key number appears on the key and on a label attached to the windscreen of a new car.

NOTE THE KEY NUMBER in your DIARY and in a reference book at HOME and then REMOVE THE LABEL FROM THE CAR. Consult your Distributor/Dealer regarding key replacements for the steering column lock.

The steering-column lock (4), if used properly, will greatly reduce the possibility of the car being stolen.

Unlocking To unlock the steering, insert the key and turn it to position 'I'. If the steering-wheel has been turned to engage the lock, slight movement of the steering-wheel will assist disengagement of the lock plunger.

With the key in the position marked 'I' the ignition is switched off and the steering lock disengaged. The heater blower motor, windscreen wipers/washers, and the radio may be operated with the key in this position. The key must be in this position when towing the car for recovery.

Ignition and start To switch on the ignition, turn the key to position 'II'. Further movement against spring resistance to position 'III' operates the starter motor. Release the key immediately the engine starts.

Locking To lock the steering, turn the key anti-clockwise to the position marked 'I', press the button (5), turn the key to the 'O' position and withdraw it.

WARNING. The steering lock/ignition/starter switch and its electrical circuits are designed to prevent the ignition system and starter from being energised while the steering lock is engaged. Serious consequences could result from alterations or substitution of the steering lock/ignition switch or its wiring. In no-circumstances must the ignition switch be separated from the steering lock.

DO NOT lubricate the steering lock/switch.

Fig. 2

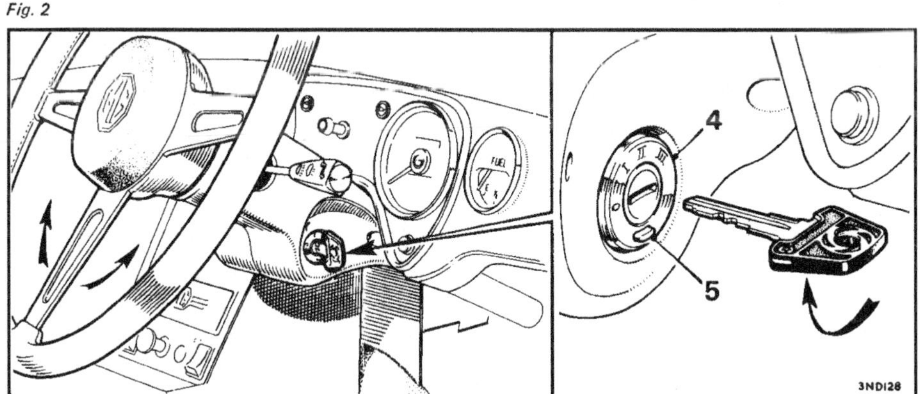

FASCIA SWITCHES Fig. 3

Blower switch and heater controls (1) For operating instructions see 'HEATING AND VENTILATING'.

Lighting switch (2) Press the lower end of the switch rocker to the first position to switch on the side and tail lamps, and to the second position to switch on the headlamps.

Panel lamp switch (3) With the side lamps switched on, illumination of the instruments may be varied by rotating the panel lamp switch knob. Turning the switch knob clockwise switches on the panel lamps; further clockwise movement of the knob reduces the light brilliance.

Fig. 3

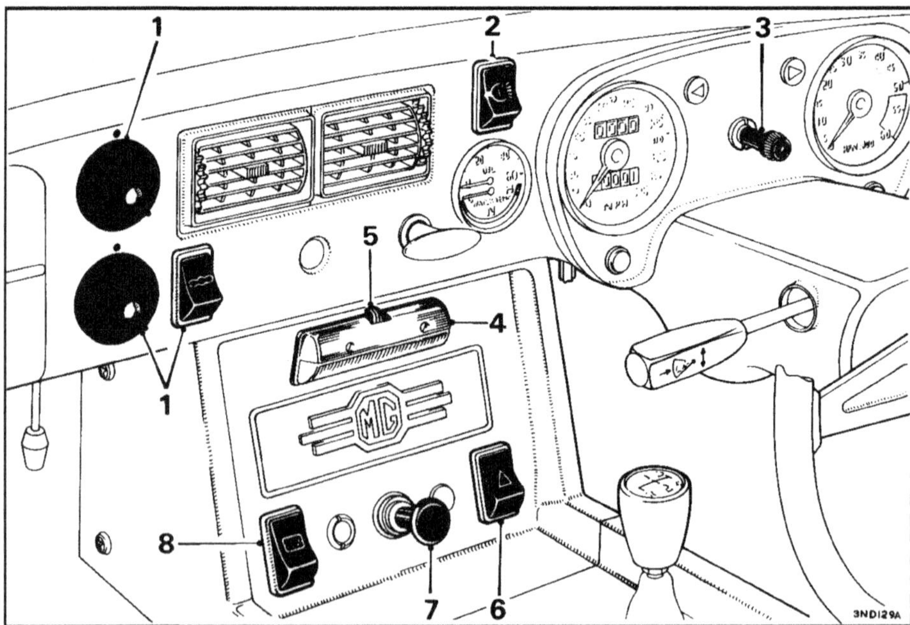

CONSOLE SWITCHES Fig. 3

Courtesy lamp (4) The courtesy lamp is controlled by the switch (5) on the lamp, and also by automatic switches operated by the front doors. With both doors closed the light may be switched on or off with the switch on the lamp.

Opening either front door will switch on the light and closing the door will extinguish it.

Hazard warning (6) To use the direction indicators as hazard warning lights, press the lower end of the switch rocker; all the direction indicators and the warning lamps will operate together, irrespective of whether the ignition is switched on or off.

Cigar-lighter (7) To operate, press the lighter knob inwards. When ready for use the lighter will partially eject itself and may then be withdrawn. The rim of the cigar-lighter is illuminated when the panel lamps are switched on.

Heated rear window (8) Press the lower end of the switch rocker to switch on the heated rear window, which will operate when the ignition is switched on. The warning lamp adjacent to the switch glows as a reminder that the heater is operating.

Refer to 'LOCKS AND BODY FITTINGS' for instructions on the care of the heated rear window.

Radio (if fitted) Full operating instructions are supplied with the radio.

STEERING COLUMN SWITCHES Fig. 4

Windscreen washer (1)
Press the knob on the end of the switch lever to operate the windscreen washer. When the windscreen is dirty, operate the washer before setting the wipers in motion.

The washer reservoir should be filled with a mixture of water and **UNIPART 'Screenwash'** solvent. It is recommended that a windscreen de-icer solvent is also added to prevent the water freezing in cold weather. On no account should radiator anti-freeze or methylated spirits (denatured alcohol) be used in the windscreen washer.

Windscreen wiper (2)
Move the switch lever down to operate the windscreen wipers at slow speed (3), further movement in the same direction will operate the wipers at fast speed (4). The wiper blades park automatically when the switch lever is returned to the off position.

Overdrive (5)
Move the lever towards the steering-wheel to engage overdrive; move the lever away from the steering-wheel to return to direct drive. For operating instructions see **'STARTING AND RUNNING INSTRUCTIONS'**.

Horn (6)
The horn is sounded by pressing the centre motif of the steering-wheel.

Direction indicators (7)
The switch is self-cancelling and operates the indicators only when the ignition is switched on. Move the lever to position (8) to operate the left-hand direction indicators and to position (9) to operate the right-hand indicators. A visual warning of a front or rear bulb failure is given when after switching on an indicator, the warning lamp and the serviceable bulb on the affected side give a continuous light.

Headlamp low beam (10)
With the headlamps switched on at the lighting switch, move the lever down away from the steering-wheel to operate the high-beam (11).

Return the lever to the midway position (10) to dip the beams.

Headlight flasher (10)
Lift the lever towards the steering-wheel (12) to flash the headlamp high-beams irrespective of whether the lighting switch is on or off.

Fig. 4

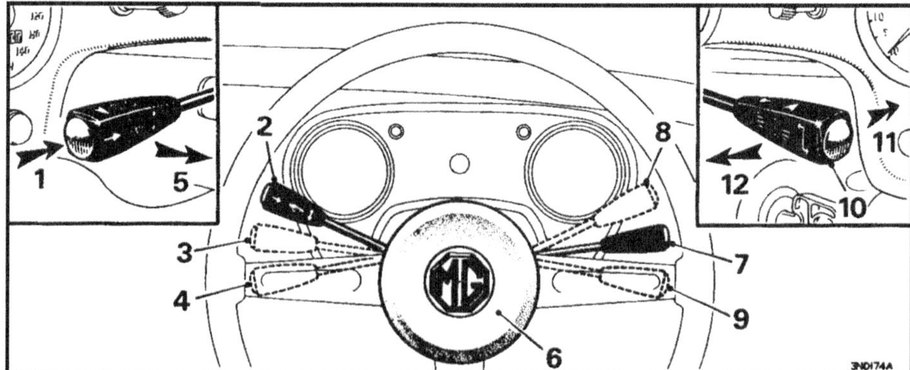

INSTRUMENTS Fig. 1

Oil pressure gauge (1) The gauge indicates the pressure of the oil in the engine lubrication system.

Temperature gauge (2) The gauge is marked 'C' (cold), 'N' (normal), and 'H' (hot), indicating the temperature of the coolant as it leaves the cooling manifold.

Speedometer (6) In addition to indicating the speed of the car, this instrument also records the total distance the car has travelled (6) and the distance travelled for any particular trip (4). To reset the trip recorder, turn the knob (5) anti-clockwise; it is important that all the counters are returned to zero.

Tachometer (7) The instrument indicates the revolutions per minute of the engine and assists the driver to use the most effective engine speed range for maximum performance in any gear.

Fuel gauge (8) When the ignition is switched on the fuel gauge needle moves slowly across the scale, taking approximately 30 seconds to indicate the amount of fuel in the tank.

Fig. 1

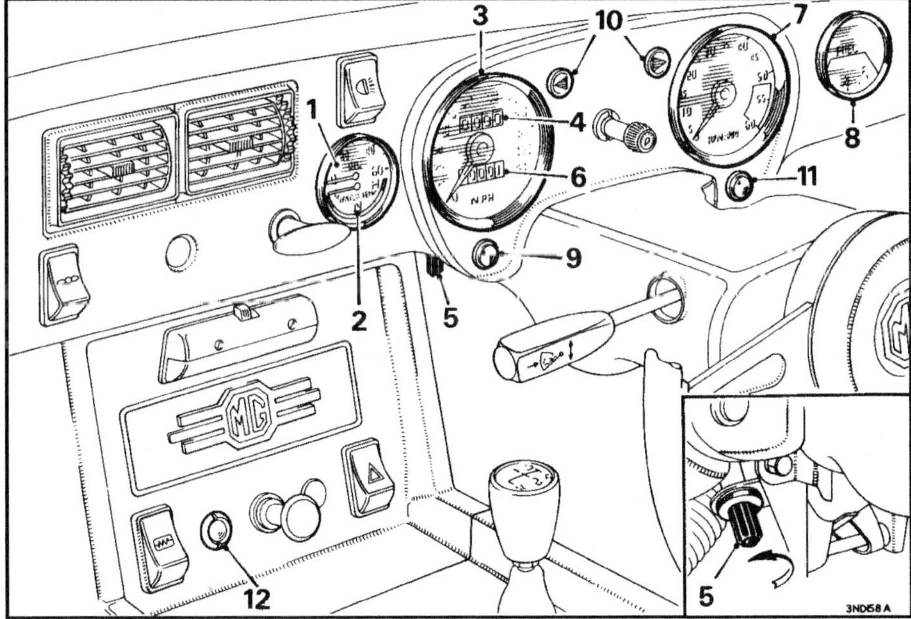

WARNING LAMPS Fig. 2

Headlamp beam —Blue (9) The lamp glows when the headlights are switched on with the beams in the high position. The light goes out when the beam is dipped.

Direction indicators —Green (10) The arrow-shaped lamps operate with the flashing direction indicators and show the direction selected.

Ignition—Red (11) The ignition warning light serves the dual purpose of reminding the driver to switch off the ignition before leaving the car and of acting as a no-charge indicator.

Heated rear window —White (12) The lamp glows when the heated rear window is switched on.

Fig. 2

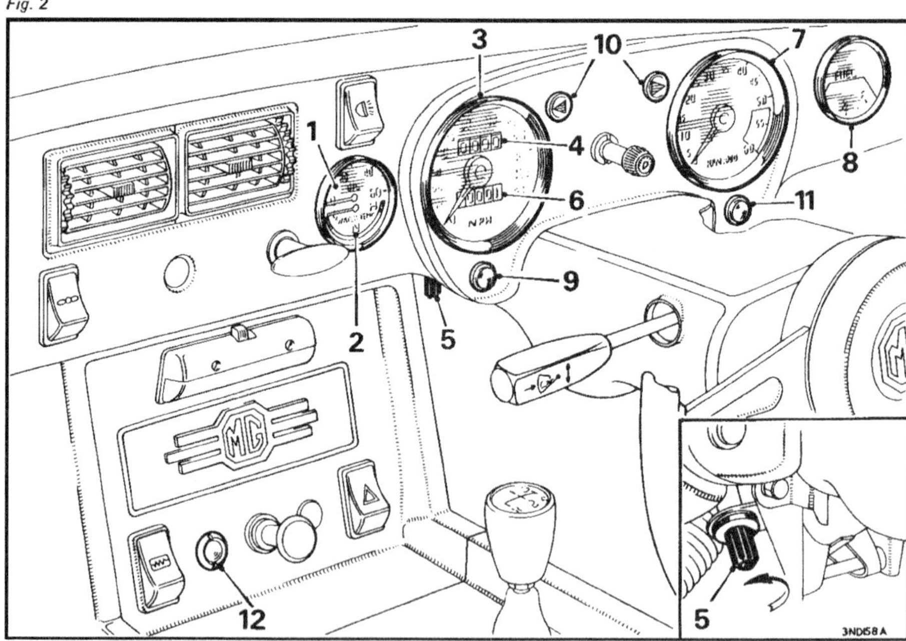

WARNING.—Exhaust fumes will be drawn into the car if it is driven with the tailgate open, causing a health hazard to passengers and driver.

If it is imperative that the car be driven with the tailgate open, adverse effects can be minimized by adopting the following procedure:

1. Close all windows.
2. Open the face vents fully.
3. Set the heater controls to circulate the maximum amount of cold or hot air.
4. Switch on the blower motor to maximum speed.
5. Do not travel at high speed.

Running in The treatment given to a new car will have an important bearing on its subsequent life, and engine speeds during this early period must be limited. The following instructions must be strictly adhered to.

During the first 500 miles:
DO NOT exceed 60 m.p.h. (90 km.p.h.).
DO NOT operate at full throttle in any gear.
DO NOT allow the engine to labour in any gear.

Choice of fuel Always use fuel with an octane rating best suited to your engine (see 'GENERAL DATA').

Filling up with fuel When filling up with fuel avoid filling the tank until fuel is visible in the filler intake tube. Should this be done and the car left in the sun, there will be a considerable risk of fuel leakage due to expansion, and consequent danger from exposed fuel. If inadvertently overfilled and the car is to be parked, take care to park it in the shade with the filler intake as high as possible

The fuel tank is vented through the filler cap. UNIPART market a lockable filler cap to fit this model.

Starting Check that the gear lever is in the neutral position.

If the engine is cold, pull out the mixture control (choke) and lock it in the desired position. In extremely cold conditions it may be necessary to pull the control out to its fullest extent.

Switch on the ignition, check that the ignition warning light glows and that the fuel gauge registers, then operate the starter.

As soon as the engine starts, release the ignition key. Check that the oil pressure gauge is registering and that the ignition warning light has gone out. Unlock the mixture control (choke) and push it in completely as soon as the engine will run evenly without its use.

Ignition warning light —Red Fig. 1

The lamp (4) should glow when the ignition is switched on and go out when the engine is started. Under certain circumstances, however, the warning lamp may still glow at engine idle speed but will go out immediately engine speed is increased. If the light does not go out, an incorrectly adjusted or broken alternator drive belt or other fault in the charging system is indicated. Driving with the lamp glowing will quickly discharge the battery, especially if other electrical units are in use.

Mixture control (choke) Fig. 1

The function of this control is to enrich the air/fuel mixture for cold engine starting and to provide a faster idle speed without enrichment during the warm-up period.

The amount which the control knob (1) must be pulled out to achieve easy starting will be dependent on engine temperature and prevailing conditions.

To lock the control in the required position, turn the control knob a quarter of a turn clockwise.

After the engine has been started with the aid of the choke, unlock the control and push it in progressively as the engine warms, until only about ½ in. (13 mm.) of travel remains (A). With the control in this position the engine will run at a faster idle speed and attain its correct working temperature as quickly as possible.

Do not warm up the engine by allowing it to idle slowly or by leaving it to idle with the control pulled out. Driving the car onto the road while the engine is cold with the control partly pulled out is preferable to allowing the engine to idle, or run with the control pulled out, in the garage or on the driveway prior to moving off.

Starter

Do not operate the starter for longer than five or six seconds.

If after a reasonable number of attempts the engine should fail to start, switch off the ignition and investigate the cause. Continued use of the starter when the engine will not start not only discharges the battery but may also damage the starter.

Fig. 1

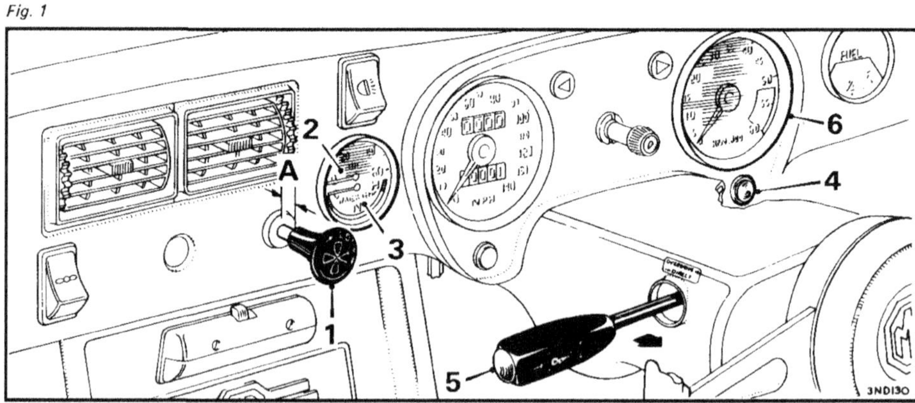

Oil pressure gauge Fig. 1	The gauge (2) should register a pressure as soon as the engine is started. Under normal running conditions and engine temperatures the pressure should be 30 to 40 lb./in.^{2} (2 to 2,8 kg./cm.^{2}).

Should the gauge fail to register any pressure, stop the engine immediately and investigate the cause. Start by checking the oil level. |

Oil pressure gauge Fig. 1

The gauge (2) should register a pressure as soon as the engine is started. Under normal running conditions and engine temperatures the pressure should be 30 to 40 lb./in.^{2} (2 to 2,8 kg./cm.^{2}).

Should the gauge fail to register any pressure, stop the engine immediately and investigate the cause. Start by checking the oil level.

Temperature gauge Fig. 1 (3)

Normal operating temperature is reached when the pointer is in the 'N' sector.

When stationary or in slow-moving traffic, the temperature will rise until the thermostatically controlled cooling fans switch on.

Should the pointer reach the 'H' sector, stop the engine and investigate the cause. Check the water pump drive belt, cooling fan operation (see page 28) and, when the system has cooled, check the coolant level.

When the ignition is switched off the needle returns to the 'C' sector.

Tachometer Fig. 1 (6)

For normal road work, and to obtain the most satisfactory service from your engine, select the appropriate gear to maintain engine speeds of between 2,000 and 4,500 r.p.m.

When maximum acceleration is required upward gear selections should be made when the needle reaches 5,000 r.p.m. Prolonged or excessive use of the highest engine speeds will tend to shorten the life of the engine. Allowing the engine to pull hard at low engine speeds must be avoided as this also has a detrimental effect on the engine.

The beginning of the red sector indicates the maximum safe speed for the engine.

Never allow the needle to enter the red sector.

Overdrive Fig. 1

The overdrive unit, controlled by a switch (5) on the steering column, provides a higher driving ratio for use with fourth gear. To engage overdrive move the switch lever towards the steering-wheel; to disengage move the lever away from the steering-wheel. Accelerator pedal pressure should be maintained and it is not necessary to depress the clutch pedal during engagement or disengagement.

Overdrive can be engaged at any throttle opening when in fourth gear. If increased acceleration is required the overdrive can be 'switched out' without alteration to the throttle setting.

DO NOT switch out the overdrive when travelling at speeds exceeding the maximum obtainable in direct drive in fourth gear.

If for any reason the overdrive does not disengage, do not reverse the car as extensive damage may result.

Vehicle loading and towing Fig. 2	The towing weight of 1,680 lb. (762 kg) is the maximum that is permissible. When using bottom gear a gradient of 1 in 6 can be ascended while towing the maximum weight. It may be necessary to adjust the maximum towing weight to comply with local conditions and regulations. The recommended downward load of a trailer or caravan on the towing hitch is 100 lb. (45 kg.), but this may be reduced or exceeded at the discretion of the driver. Any load carried on the roof or downward load from a towing hitch must also be included in the maximum loading of the vehicle.
Roof rack Fig. 2	Bulky rather than heavy **loads no greater than 50 lb. (23 kg) may be carried on a roof rack.** Any load on the roof may affect the handling of the car, especially in a cross-wind or when cornering. Use the **Unipart** roof rack.
Wet brakes	If the car has been washed, driven through water, or over wet roads for prolonged periods full braking power may not be available. Dry the brakes by applying the foot brake lightly several times while the car is in motion. Keep the hand brake applied while using high-pressure washing equipment.
On-tow for recovery	Should it become necessary to tow the car, use the towing-eyes provided. For recovery the car should be towed with the key in the ignition/steering lock at position 'I'. For tow starting the key should be at position 'II'. Unipart market an approved Emergency Towing Strap and have designed a towing bracket and full electrical kit for your vehicle. Be safe, be sure and fit **Unipart** towing accessories.

Fig. 2

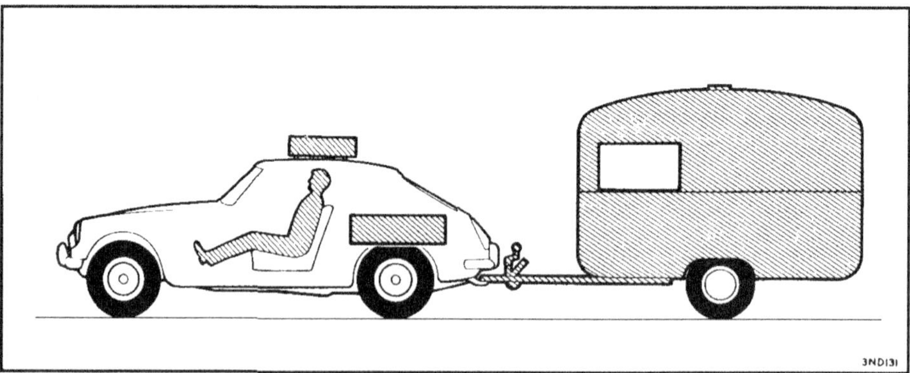

Key number Two keys and a duplicate set are provided, the large key for the steering lock and ignition switch and the small key for the front doors, glove box and trunk lid.

In order to reduce the possibility of theft, **locks are not marked with a number. NOTE THE KEY NUMBERS IMMEDIATELY on taking delivery of the car**—see page 5.

Window regulators
Fig. 1 To open a door window, turn the handle regulator (1) to obtain the opening required.

Door locks
Fig. 1 Both front doors may be locked from outside the car with the small key provided, and locked from inside the car with door locking catch.

To unlock the front doors from the outside, insert the key into the lock and turn it towards the front of the car, return it to the upright position and withdraw it. Grasp the handle and depress the button (2) to open the door.

To lock the front doors from the outside, turn the key towards the rear of the car, return it to the upright position and withdraw it.

To lock the doors from inside the car, close the door and move the locking latch (3) towards the rear of the car. To open the doors, move the locking latch towards the front of the car and pull the release lever (4) rearwards. The doors can be opened from the outside when the locking latch is in the forward position. The locking latch cannot be set to the lock position while the door is open.

Fig. 1

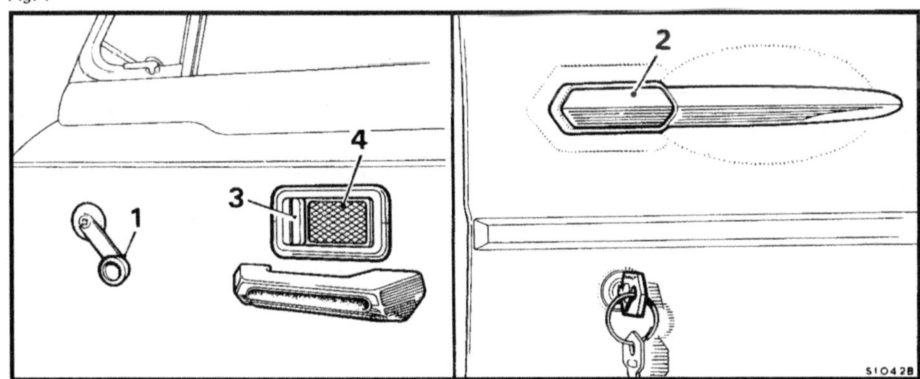

Glovebox
Fig. 2

To **unlock,** insert the small key and turn it anti-clockwise.

To **lock,** turn the key clockwise.

The glovebox lid must be locked with the key to retain it in the closed position.

Trunk lid
Fig. 3

To **unlock,** insert the small key into the lock and turn the key anti-clockwise.

To **open,** depress the lock plunger (1) and raise the lid. Raising the trunk lid automatically switches on the interior light. Springs retain the lid in the open position.

To **close,** lower the trunk lid.

To **lock,** turn the key clockwise and withdraw it.

Fig. 2

Fig. 3

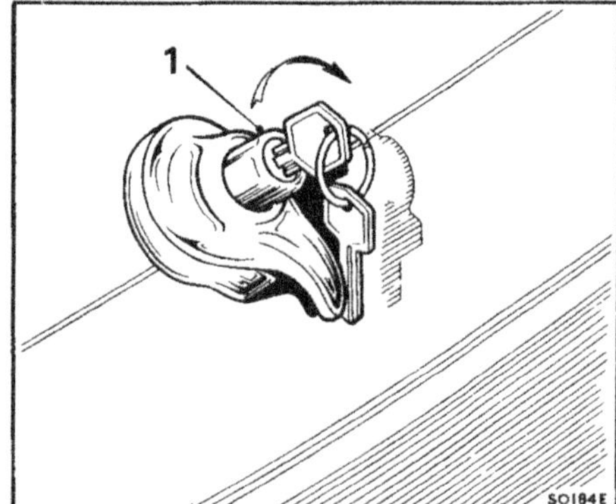

Fig. 4

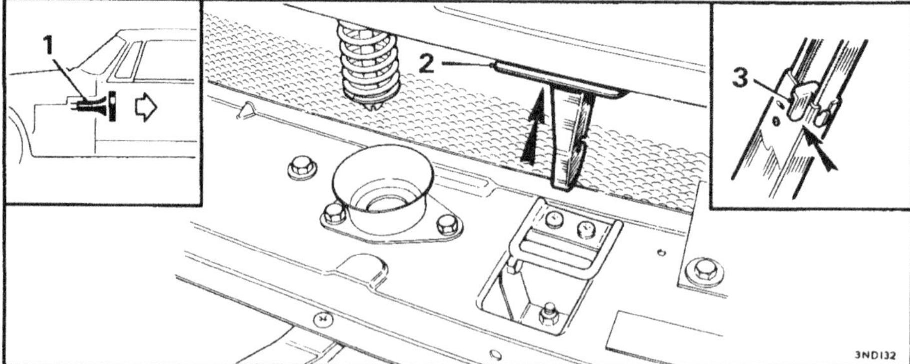

Bonnet Fig. 4	**To open,** pull the knob (1) located inside the car on the left-hand side below the fascia panel.

Bonnet
Fig. 4

To open, pull the knob (1) located inside the car on the left-hand side below the fascia panel.

Outside the car at the bonnet, press up the safety catch (2) under the front of the bonnet, and raise the bonnet. As the bonnet is raised the support stay will automatically spring into engagement and hold the bonnet open.

To close, raise the bonnet slightly, push the catch (3) on the bonnet stay rearwards to release the locking mechanism, and lower the bonnet. Apply light pressure with the palms of the hands at the front corners of the bonnet and press down quickly; undue force is not necessary and may cause damage. The safety catch and lock will be heard to engage.

Front ventilator windows
Fig. 5

To open, move the catch lever (1) upwards and push the window outwards.

To close, pull the catch inwards, and then push it forward until the catch is in the locked position.

Rear ventilator windows
Fig. 6

To open, pull the catch (1) forward and then push the catch outwards.

To close, pull the centre of the catch inwards and then push it backwards until the catch snaps over into the locked position.

Lubrication

To ensure trouble–free operation it is essential that the locks, hinges and catches are adequately lubricated.

Locks. Inject a small quantity of thin oil, preferably **Unipart Lockspray,** through the key slots and around the push-buttons. **Do not** oil the steering lock.

Hinges. Apply grease or oil to the joints of the hinges.

Bonnet catches. Apply grease to the moving surfaces of the bonnet release mechanism and oil to the release lever and safety-catch pivot points.

Fig. 5

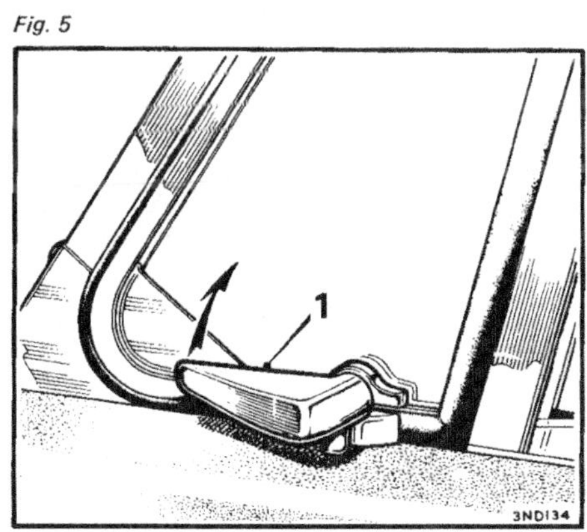

Fig. 6

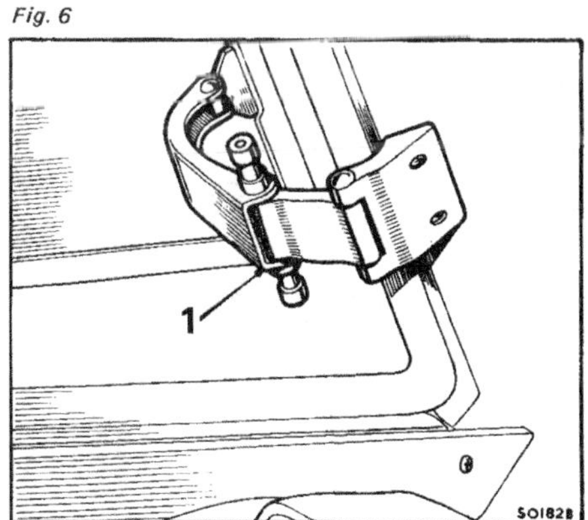

Mirrors
Fig. 7

Interior. The mirror stem is designed to break away from the mounting bracket on impact. The stem may be refitted in the mounting bracket as follows. Align the stem ball (1) with the bracket cup (2), ensuring that the small protrusion (3) on the stem aligns with the indent of the mounting bracket. Give them a smart tap with a soft instrument to join the two components.

Set the mirror head for daylight rear view with the anti-dazzle lever (4) down away from the windscreen. During night driving, if dazzled, move the anti-dazzle lever forward towards the windscreen.

Exterior. The mirror (5) may be adjusted from the seat position when the window is open.

Arm-rest and
ashtray
Fig. 8

To gain access to the compartment below the arm-rest, raise the forward end of the arm-rest. To empty the ash tray, raise the lid (1) and remove the ash tray by lifting under the stubber (2).

Do not attempt to remove the ashtray by pulling on the lid.

Fig. 7

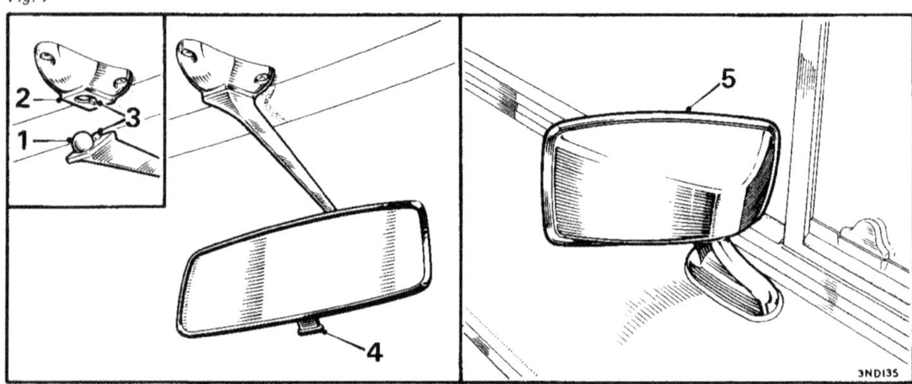

Fig. 8

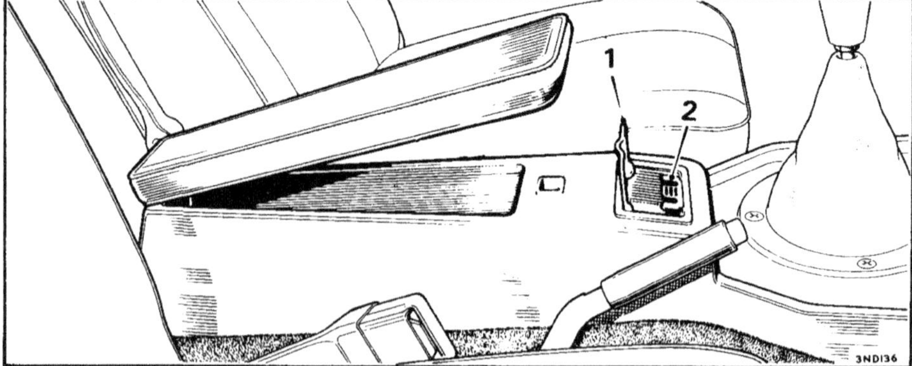

Periodic examination of the drain holes should be made to ensure that they are clear of obstruction; use a piece of stiff wire to probe the apertures.

Careless application of underseal can result in restricted drainage. Masking tape or plugs used when underseal is being applied must be removed immediately the operation is completed.

Jacking up beneath the underfloor may deform the drain apertures; always use the jacking points provided.

Fig. 9

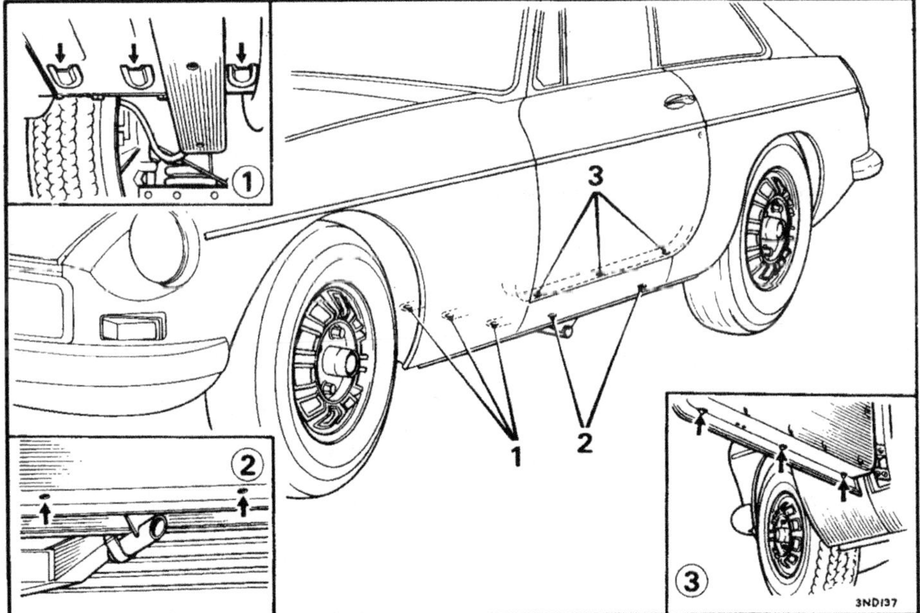

Heated rear window
Fig. 10

The heated rear window has a heating element (arrowed) on the surface of the glass and with reasonable care will last indefinitely.

The following practices will damage the circuit and must be avoided.

1. Scratching off labels and advertising stickers.
2. Wiping the glass with the back of a ringed hand.
3. Stowing hard and metal objects so that they abrade the glass.
4. Cleaning with harsh abrasives.

Increased luggage area
Fig. 10

To increase the luggage capacity the back of the rear seat can be folded down.

Release the locks by moving the catch handles (1) downwards and moving the back of the seat (2) forward.

To return the seat to the normal position, lift the seat and lock in position by moving the catch handles upwards.

Fig. 10

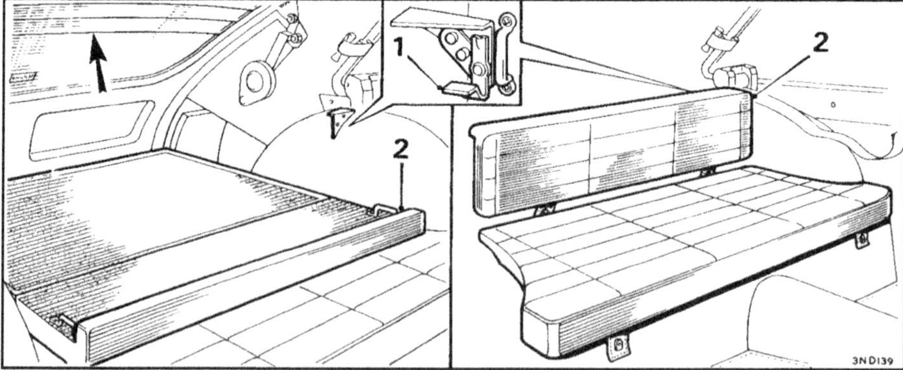

Seat adjustment
Fig. 1

Front seats can be moved forwards or backwards if the lever (1) located beneath the front of each seat is pressed outwards; hold the lever in this position while the seat position is adjusted. The locking pin is spring-loaded and will automatically lock the seat in the required position when the lever is released.

Adjustable back-rest
Fig. 1

The angle of the seat back-rest may also be adjusted by easing the body weight from the seat back-rest, and moving the lever (2) in the direction of the arrow. Release the lever and ensure the seat is locked in position by applying back pressure.

Access to rear seats
Fig. 1

Move the seat catch (3) forward, and fold the back of the front seat forwards. The catch will automatically re-engage when the rear of the seat is moved back to the correct driving position.

Head restraint
Fig. 1

The head restraint (4) may be raised or lowered as desired.

Fig. 1

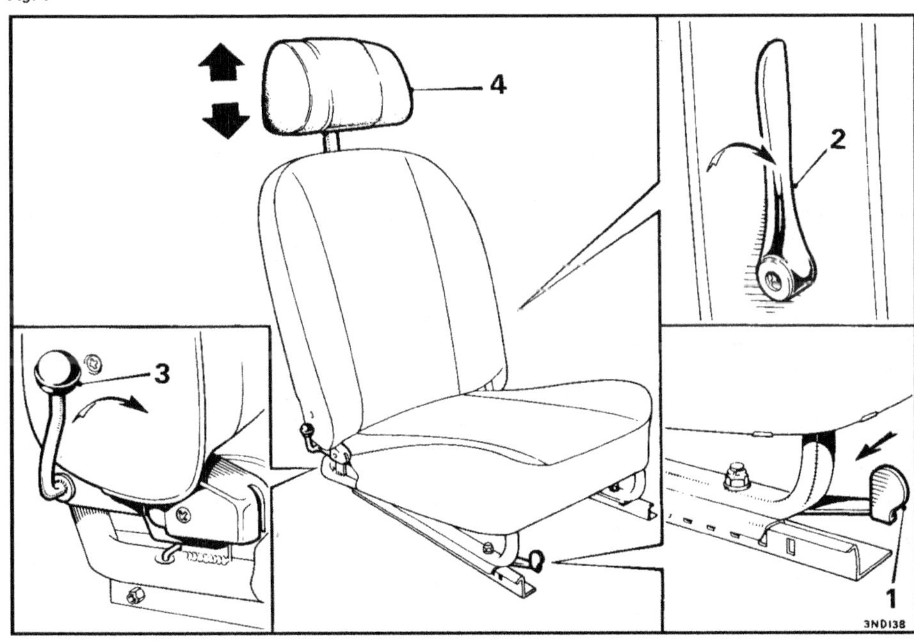

Wearing
Fig. 1

Always ensure that the belt is lying flat and is not twisted either on the wearer's body or between the wearer and the anchorage point. Never at any time wear a belt loosely as this reduces its protection.

Never attempt to wear the belt other than as a complete diagonal and lap assembly. Do not try to use the belt for more than one person at any one time, even children.

The reel (1) of the automatic belt allows the wearer freedom for normal movements. Hard braking or fast cornering of the vehicle immediately locks the belt.

To fasten, lift the engagement tongue (2) and draw the belt from the automatic reel over the shoulder and across the chest, and push it into the locking clip (3) of the short belt nearest the wearer.

To release, press the release button (4) on the short belt.

Allow the webbing to retract into the automatic reel. Ensure that when the belt is retracted the engagement tongue (2) has not moved on the belt to a point near the sill mounting; this can be remedied by moving the tongue and belt clip (5) towards the reel.

To stow, place the engagement tongue (2) into the stowing pocket (6) mounted under the rear ventilator windows.

Fig. 1

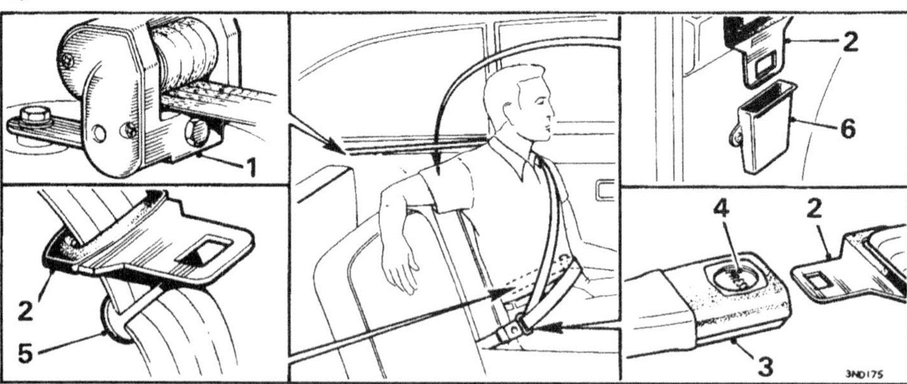

Care of the
belts No unauthorized alterations or additions to the belt should be made. Inspect the webbing periodically for signs of abrasions, cuts, fraying, and general wear; pay particular attention to the fixing points and adjusters. Replace belts that are defective or have been subjected to severe strain.

Do not attempt to bleach the belt webbing or re-dye it. If the belt becomes soiled, sponge with warm water using a non-detergent soap and allow to dry naturally.

Do not use caustic soap, chemical cleaners or detergents for cleaning: do not dry with artificial heat or by direct exposure to the sun.

Fresh air
Fig. 1

Fresh air is admitted to the car for cooling and ventilation through an adjustable vent mounted behind the centre console.

Air enters the car interior through the two doors located one each side of the gearbox tunnel in the foot wells.

The flow of air may be adjusted by moving the control knob (1) backwards to one of the three open positions; move the knob to the most forward position to close the vent.

Face-level vents
Fig. 1

Air flow for cooling and ventilation from the face-level vents mounted on the fascia panel may be adjusted by turning the serrated control wheel (2) on the outer side of each vent. Move the wheel downwards to open.

The direction of the air flow is adjusted by moving the shutter control knob (3) mounted in the centre of each vent.

Fig. 1

<table>
<tr><td>Fresh-air
heater
Fig. 2</td><td>The heating and ventilating system is designed to provide fresh air either heated by the engine cooling system or at outside temperature to the car at floor level and for demisting and defrosting to the windscreen. Full heat output is not available until the engine has reached normal operating temperature.

Air distribution for heating is independent of the fresh-air system; the control knob (1) (in Fig. 1) should be in the closed position when heated air is being distributed.</td></tr>
<tr><td>Heater
controls
Fig. 2</td><td>Air temperature. Turn the knob (1) in the direction of the arrow to raise the air temperature.

Air flow. Turn the knob (2) in the direction of the arrow to the position marked on the control to direct the air distribution.

Booster fan. Press the lower half of the rocker switch (3) down to switch on the air flow booster.

Use the booster when the car is stationary, moving at a slow speed or to augment the air supply in adverse weather conditions.</td></tr>
<tr><td>Usage</td><td>The heater and air flow controls may be set at the position marked on the control knobs or to any other intermediate positions. By varying the control settings, and utilizing the booster blower, a wide range of settings can be obtained to suit prevailing conditions.</td></tr>
</table>

Fig. 2

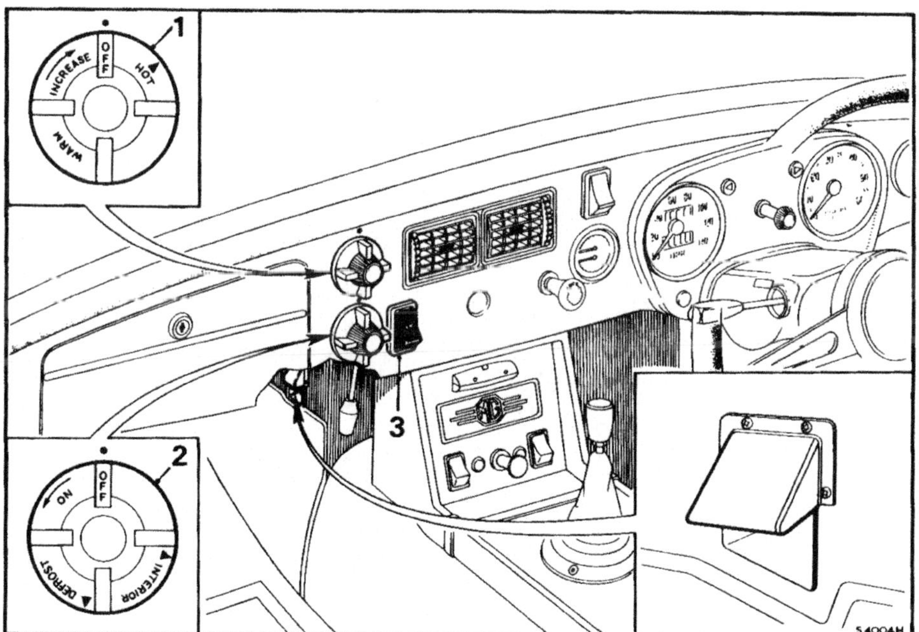

Coolant   Water alone must not be used in the cooling system as this could have a detrimental effect on the aluminium engine components.

An anti-freeze solution conforming to specification BS 3150 must be used to protect the coolant passages against corrosion and also give frost protection.

When topping up, a mixture of anti-freeze and water must always be used.

Expansion tank and cap
Fig. 1   The expansion tank collects the coolant displaced by expansion when the engine is heated to normal running temperature. The displaced coolant is returned to the radiator when the system cools. The cap (1) on the expansion tank maintains the pressure in the cooling system at 15 lb./in.^{2} (1 kg/cm^2.) maximum when the engine is running.

To remove the cap. If the system is hot, protect the hands against escaping steam, and turn the cap anti-clockwise to the stop, wait until the pressure has escaped, press down and turn further until the cap can be lifted off.

Checking
Fig. 1   The coolant level must only be checked when the system is **cold.** Remove the expansion tank cap (1) to check the coolant level, which must be maintained so that the expansion tank is half full.

Fig. 1

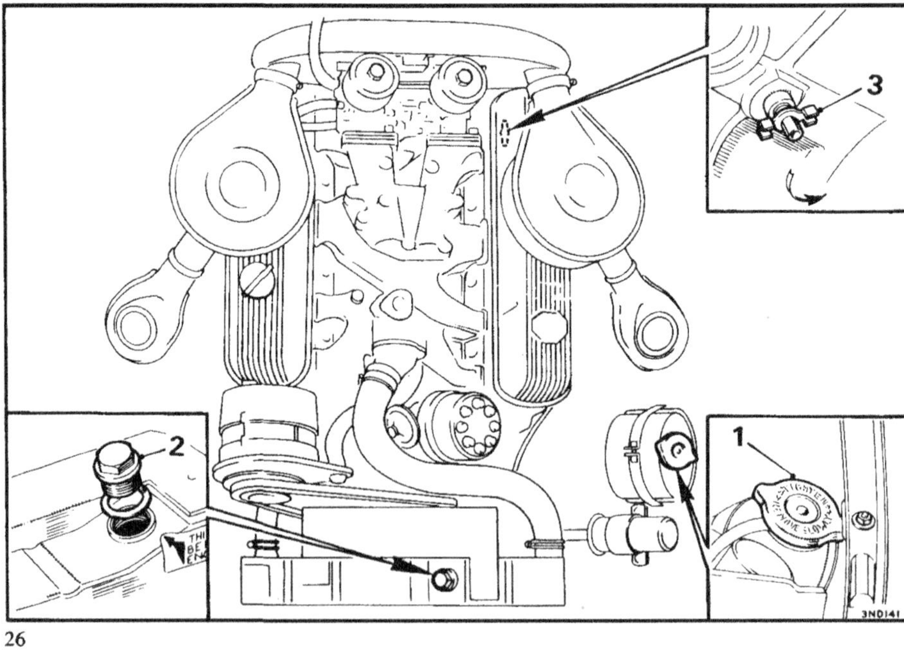

<table>
<tr><td style="vertical-align:top; text-align:right; width:18%">Draining
Fig. 1</td><td>As injury could be caused by escaping steam or water the radiator filler plug (2) must not be removed while the system is hot.

To drain the cooling system, stand the car on level ground, remove the expansion tank cap (1) and the radiator filler plug (2). Slacken the hose clip and disconnect the bottom hose from the radiator. To drain the engine, open the drain tap (3) on the left-hand side of the cylinder block.

Owing to the location of the car heater and the expansion tank they cannot be drained with the cooling system.</td></tr>
</table>

<table>
<tr><td style="vertical-align:top; text-align:right; width:18%">Filling
Fig. 1</td><td>Refit the bottom hose and close the engine drain tap. Check that all hose connections are tight. Turn the heater temperature control knob to 'HOT' to open the heater valve.

Fill the system through the radiator filler and bring the level up to the bottom of the threads. Refit the filler plug (2).

Top up the coolant in the expansion tank so that the tank is half-full. Refit the cap (1).

Start up and run the engine until the top radiator hose is warm and switch off the engine.

Turn the expansion tank cap to its safety stop to release the pressure.

Remove the radiator filler plug and top up once more to the bottom of the threads. Refit the filler plug. Top up the expansion tank to half-full.</td></tr>
</table>

<table>
<tr><td style="vertical-align:top; text-align:right; width:18%">Frost precautions</td><td>Water expands when it freezes, and if precautions are not taken there is considerable risk of bursting the radiator, cylinder block, or heater. The heater unit cannot be drained with the cooling system; it is therefore essential to use anti-freeze in the cooling system in freezing conditions.

We recommend the use of Bluecol 'U' universal anti-freeze to protect the cooling system.

If Bluecol 'U' universal is not available any anti-freeze conforming to specification B.S. 3150 may be used. Anti-freeze to this specification is compatible with Bluecol 'U' universal and can be used with it. Bluecol 'U' universal should not be mixed with other universal anti-freezes.

After filling with anti-freeze solution, attach a warning label in a prominent position on the car stating the type of anti-freeze contained in the cooling system to ensure that the correct type is used for topping-up.

Anti-freeze can remain in the cooling system for two years provided that the specific gravity of the coolant is checked periodically and anti-freeze added as necessary. The specific gravity check should be carried out by an authorized Distributor or Dealer. After the second year the system should be drained and flushed by inserting a hose in the filling orifice and allowing water to flow through until clean. Make sure that the cooling system is water-tight, examine all joints and replace any defective hose with a new one. Refill with the appropriate anti-freeze solution and add 0.25 pint ($\frac{1}{3}$ U.S. pint, 0.15 litre) of neat anti-freeze to the expansion tank.</td></tr>
</table>

The recommended quantities of anti-freeze solution are given below.

Solution	Amount of anti-freeze		Commences freezing		Frozen solid	
%	Pints	Litres	°C	°F	°C	°F
25	4	2	−13	9	−26	−15
33⅓	5½	3.25	−19	−2	−36	−33
50	8	4.5	−36	−33	−48	−53

Do not use radiator anti-freeze solution in the windscreen-washing equipment. Use the correct washer solvent, which will not damage the paintwork.

Cooling fans
Fig. 2

The electrically driven radiator cooling fans (1) are controlled by a thermostatic switch (2) in the top of the induction manifold. During normal driving the fans will operate infrequently, but driving at slow speeds, or running the engine when stationary will cause the fans to operate more often.

Checking. With the ignition switched on, pull the connector (3) from the thermostatic switch (2). The fans should operate when the connector is earthed (4). Reconnect the lead, start and run the engine until the fans operate. Should the fans not operate when earthed, or before the temperature gauge reaches 'H', consult your Distributor or Dealer.

Fig. 2

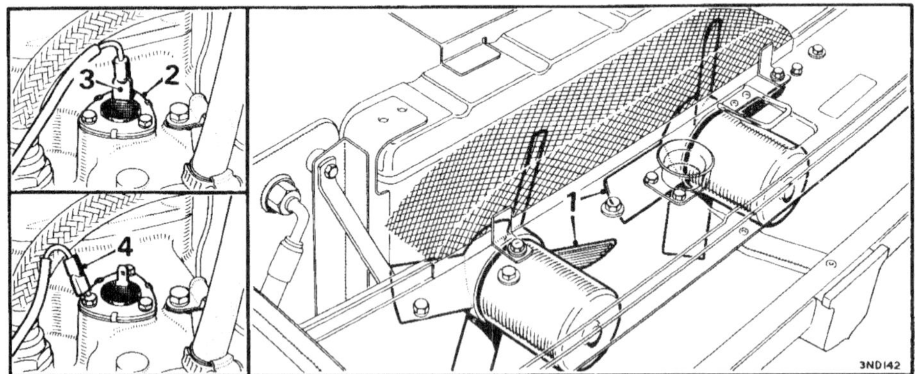

WHEELS AND TYRES

Care of the jack Neglect of the jack may lead to difficulty in a roadside emergency. Examine it occasionally, clean off accumulated dust, and lightly oil the thread to prevent corrosion.

Jacking up
Fig. 1 The jack is designed to lift one side of the car at a time. Apply the hand brake, and chock the wheels on the opposite side to that being jacked; use a wood block jammed tight against the tyre tread.

Insert the lifting arm (2) of the jack into the socket located in the door sill panel. **Make certain that the jack lifting arm is pushed fully into the socket and that the base of the jack is on firm ground.** The jack should lean slightly outwards at the top to allow for the radial movement of the car as it is raised.

WARNING.–Do not work beneath the vehicle with the lifting jack as the sole means of support. Place suitable supports under the front side-members or rear axle to give adequate support and safety while working.

ROAD WHEELS

Preventive
maintenance Owners are recommended to check wheel nuts for tightness each week in addition to checking the other items listed on page 64. Take care not to overtighten (see 'GENERAL DATA')..

Removing
Fig. 1 Apply the hand brake and take the weight of the car with the jack and slacken the wheel nuts (3). Raise the car with the jack to lift the wheel clear of the ground and remove the nuts (3). Remove the road wheel.

Refitting
Fig. 1 Fit the wheel onto the wheel studs. Screw on the nuts, ensuring the spigot (arrowed) of each nut engages in the stud hole of the wheel and lightly tighten the nuts. Lower the jack and tighten the nuts progressively in a diagonal sequence (see **'GENERAL DATA'**). Remove the jack.

Fig. 1

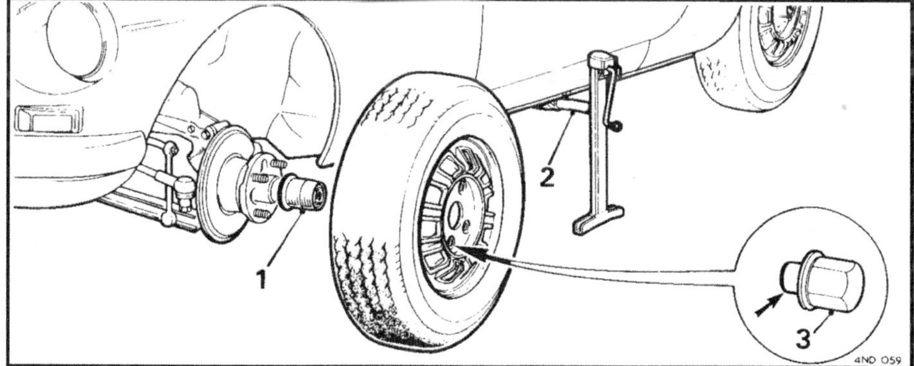

Centre cap
Figs. 1 and 2

To remove **the centre cap (1)**, jack up the car and remove the wheel. Wipe the centre cap clean. Place the wheel on the ground with the centre cap face upwards and press the centre cap out of the wheel in the direction indicated by the arrow.

To **refit the centre cap,** insert it into the wheel (from the inside). Lay the wheel on the ground, outer face down, and press the centre cap into the wheel. Refit the wheel, lower the car and remove the jack.

Spare wheel location
Fig. 3

The spare wheel is stowed in the well of the luggage compartment beneath the luggage platform floor.

To gain access to the spare wheel, turn back the luggage compartment floor covering, unscrew the two quick-release screws (1) and lift the floorboard (2). Unscrew the clamp plate (3) to release the spare wheel.

When refitting position the wheel face down in the well of the luggage compartment and retain in position with the clamp plate.

TYRES AND TYRE PRESSURES

Replacements

Radial-ply tubeless tyres are standard equipment. The permissible load and tyre pressures are given in **'GENERAL DATA'**.

Replacement tyres must be to the recommended specification as given in **'GENERAL DATA'** and of the radial-ply type.

Tyre pressures

Owners are reminded that tyre wear and inflation pressures are subject to legal requirements; check the tyre pressures weekly including the spare, using a **UNIPART Tyre Pressure Gauge.** If necessary, use a **UNIPART Foot Pump** to increase the pressures to the recommendations given in **'GENERAL DATA'**. The tyres should also be inspected at frequent intervals for damage and wear.

On new cars the spare wheel is inflated above the recommended pressure and it must be checked and adjusted before use.

Fig. 2

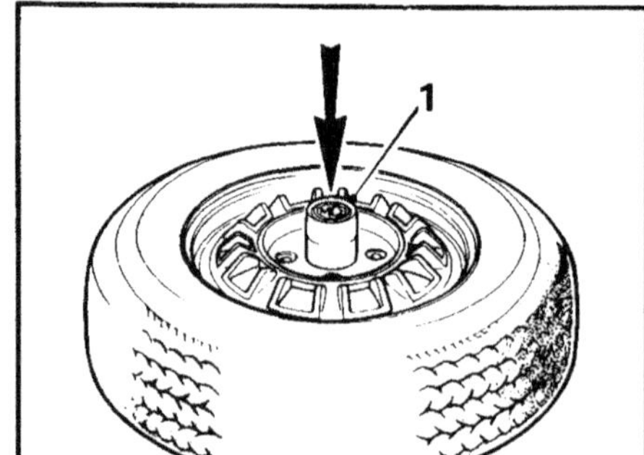

Fig. 3

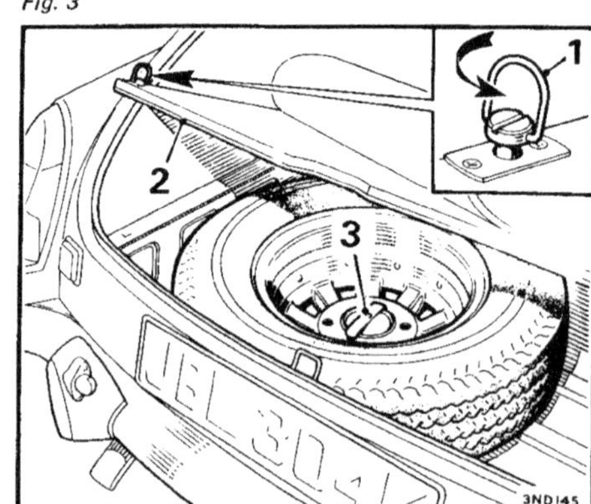

Pressures should be checked when the tyres are cold, and should not be reduced in warm tyres when the increase above normal pressure is due to temperature. Tyres are permeable and a natural pressure loss will occur with time. The pressure loss in a week should be no more than 2 lb./sq. in. (0.14 kg./cm.^{2}); any unusual pressure loss should be investigated.

Under-inflation is hazardous and causes rapid tyre wear, possibly causing permanent damage to the cords of the tyre casing due to excessive flexing of the cover walls.

Valves and caps See that the valve caps are screwed down firmly by hand. Do not use tools as too much force will damage the rubber seating. The cap prevents the entry of dirt into the valve mechanism and forms an additional seal on the valve.

Tyre care The tyres should also be inspected at frequent intervals for damage and wear. Excessive local distortion as a result of striking a kerb, a loose brick, a deep pot-hole, etc., may cause the casing cords to fracture. Every effort should be made to avoid such obstacles.

Any oil or grease which may get onto the tyres should be cleaned off, using petrol (fuel) sparingly. Do not use paraffin (kerosene), which has a detrimental effect on rubber.

Flints and other sharp objects should be removed with a penknife or similar tool. If neglected, they may work through the tyre.

Repairs Normally a tubeless tyre will not leak as a result of penetration by a nail or other puncturing object, provided that it is left in the tyre. At a convenient time have the tyre removed for vulcanizing. If a small diameter puncture has been made a temporary repair can be carried out with the tyre manufacturer's plugging kit.

NOTE.–The insertion of a plug to repair a puncture in a tubeless tyre must be regarded as a temporary measure and a **permanent vulcanized repair must be made as soon as possible.** In no circumstances should a plug repair be made to the side wall of a tyre.

The instructions given for the temporary repair of tubeless tyres must be disregarded when tubes are fitted. If in any doubt, consult your Distributor or Dealer.

Wheel and tyre balancing Unbalanced wheel and tyre assemblies may be responsible for abnormal wear of the tyres and vibration in the steering. Consult your Distributor/Dealer.

Front brake pads
Fig. 1

Wear on the disc brake friction pads (arrowed) is automatically compensated for during braking operations and manual adjustment is therefore not required.

If the wear on one pad is greater than on the other their operating positions should be changed over by your Distributor or Dealer.

Remove the road wheel to gain clear access to the pads for inspection.

The pads must be renewed when the lining material has worn to the minimum permissible thickness of $\frac{1}{16}$ in. (1.6 mm.) or will have done so before the next regular inspection is due. Special equipment is required to renew the brake pads; this work should be entrusted to your Distributor or Dealer.

After fitting new pads, within the limits of safety, heavy braking should be avoided for a few days to allow the pads to bed-in.

Rear brakes
Fig. 2

Excessive brake pedal travel is an indication that the rear brake-shoes require adjusting. The brake-shoes on both rear wheels must be adjusted to regain even and efficient braking.

Adjusting. Chock the front wheels, fully release the hand brake and jack up each rear wheel in turn placing suitable supports beneath the vehicle—see 'WARNING' on page 29. Turn the adjuster (1) in a clockwise direction (viewed from the centre of the car), using a **UNIPART Brake Adjusting Spanner** until the brake-shoes lock the wheel, then turn the adjuster back until the wheel is free to rotate without the shoes rubbing. Repeat the adjustment on the other rear brake.

Hand brake
Fig. 2

The hand brake is automatically adjusted with the rear brakes. If there is excessive movement of the hand brake lever, consult your Distributor or Dealer. To lubricate charge the nipple (2) on the hand brake cable with one of the recommended greases.

Fig. 1

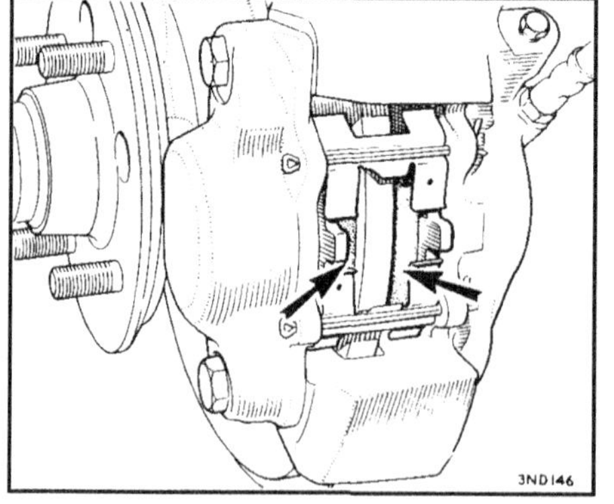

Fig. 2

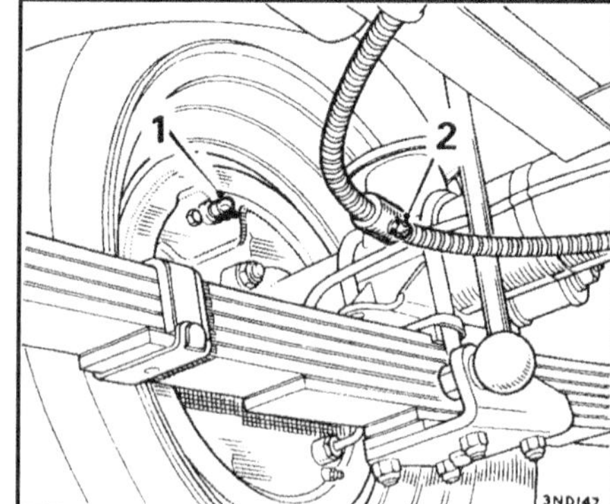

Inspecting rear brake linings
Fig. 3

Chock the front wheels and release the hand brake. Jack up each rear wheel in turn, placing suitable supports beneath the vehicle—see **'WARNING'** on page 29.

Remove the road wheel and slacken the brake-shoe adjuster fully.

Remove the two countersunk screws (1) and withdraw the brake-drum (2).

Inspect the linings (3) for wear, and clean the dust from the backplate assembly and drum preferably using methylated spirit (denatured alcohol). Brake lining dust is dangerous to health if inhaled and therefore should not be blown from the drums. Make certain that sufficient lining material remains to allow the car to run until the next regular inspection is due without the thickness falling below the safe limit.

Refit the brake drums and the road wheels and adjust the brake-shoes (see page 32).

Brake pedal
Fig. 4

A free movement of $\frac{1}{8}$ in. (3 mm.) (A), measured at the pedal pad must be maintained on the pedal. To adjust the free movement, slacken the stop light switch locknut (1) and turn the switch (2) clockwise to decrease or anti-clockwise to increase the clearance. Tighten the stop light switch locknut.

Replacing brake shoes and pads

When it becomes necessary to renew the brake-shoes or pads it is essential that only **genuine** replacements, with the correct grade of lining, are used. Always fit new shoes as complete axle sets, never individually or as a single wheel set. Serious consequences could result from out-of-balance braking due to mixing of linings.

Replacement brake-shoes are obtainable from your Distributor or Dealer under the **Service Exchange Scheme**, see page 72.

Fig. 3

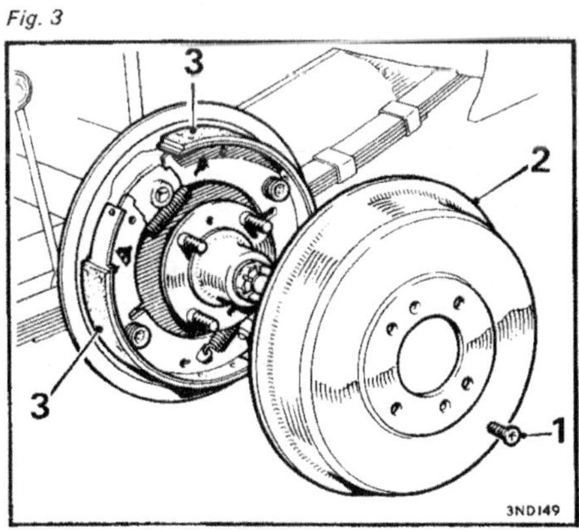

Fig. 4

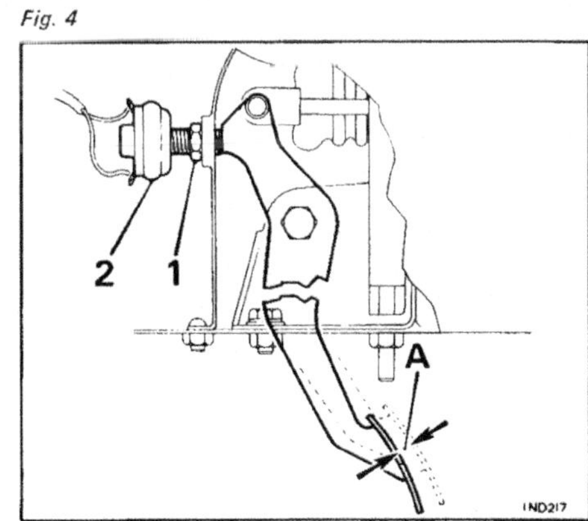

<table>
<tr><td>

Brake and clutch master cylinder
Fig. 5

</td><td>

To check the level of the fluid in the brake (1) and clutch (2) master cylinder reservoirs, remove the plastic filler caps.

The fluid level must be maintained at ½ in. (13 mm.) below the bottom of the filler cap.

</td></tr>
</table>

Top up if necessary with **UNIPART 550 Brake fluid**; alternatively use a high-boiling-point brake fluid conforming to specification S.A.E. J1703c with a minimum boiling point of 260°C (500°F). **DO NOT use any other type of fluid.** Frequent topping-up is indicative of a leak in the system which must be checked and the leak rectified immediately.

Before refitting the filler caps, separate the dome (3) from the filler cap and check that the breather holes, indicated by arrows, are clear. Snap fit the dome onto the filler cap.

NOTE.—Brake fluid can have a detrimental effect on paintwork. Ensure that fluid is not allowed to contact paint-finished surfaces.

Servo filter
Fig. 6

The filter should be cleaned at the recommended intervals with compressed air at low pressure. Do not use cleaning fluid or lubricant of any description on the filter.

Removing the filter. Lever the dome (1) off the valve cover, remove and clean the filter (2).

When refitting, make sure that the air valve spring (3) is securely located onto the valve, refit the filter (2) and snap-fit the dome (1) onto the valve cover.

Fig. 5

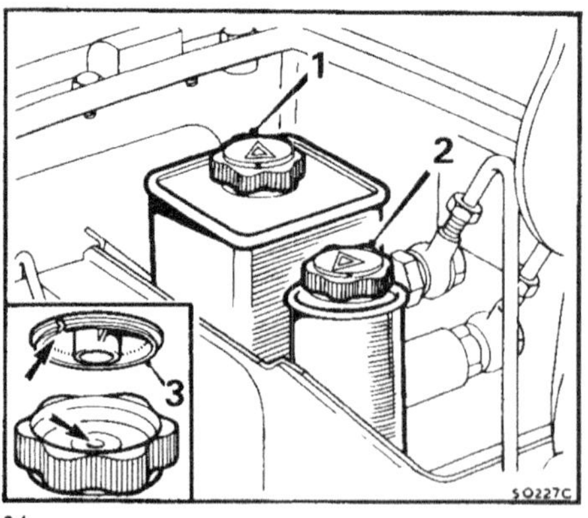

Fig. 6

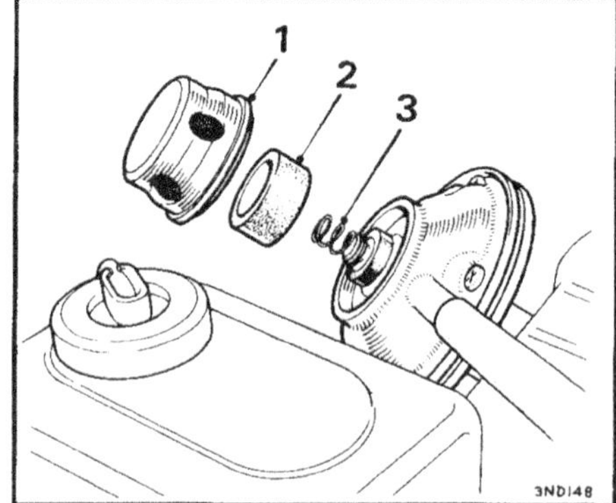

Visual check   Examine the clutch and brake hoses, pipes, unions, and joints for tightness and general condition. It is most important to ensure that no chafing of connections or pipes develops at any time, and that leakages are rectified immediately.

Preventive maintenance   In addition to the recommended periodical inspection of brake components it is advisable as the car ages and as a precaution against the effects of wear and deterioration, to make a more searching inspection and renew parts as necessary.

It is recommended that:

(1) Disc brake pads, drum brake linings, hoses, and pipes should be examined at intervals no greater than those laid down in the Passport to Service.

(2) Brake fluid should be changed completely every 18 months or 18,000 miles (30000 km.) whichever is the sooner.

(3) All fluid seals in the hydraulic system should be renewed, and all flexible hoses should be examined and renewed if necessary every 3 years or 36,000 miles (60000 km.) whichever is the sooner. At the same time the working surface of the piston and of the bores of the master cylinder, wheel cylinders, and other slave cylinders should be examined and new parts fitted where necessary.

Care must be taken always to observe the following points:

(a) At all times use the recommended brake fluid.

(b) Never leave fluid in unsealed containers. It absorbs moisture quickly and this can be dangerous if used in the braking system.

(c) Fluid drained from the system or used for bleeding is best discarded.

(d) The necessity for absolute cleanliness throughout cannot be over-emphasized.

POLARITY The electrical installation on this car is **NEGATIVE** (–) earth return and the correct polarity must be maintained at all times. Reversed polarity will permanently damage semi-conductor devices in the alternator and tachometer, and the transistors in the radio (if fitted).

Before fitting a radio or any other electrical equipment, make certain that it has the correct polarity for installation in this vehicle.

BATTERIES

Access
Fig. 1 Unlock the seat catches and move the back of the rear seat forward. Release the rear seat cushion securing straps from the fasteners, and pull the cushion forward.

Remove the carpet covering the rear compartment floor. Turn the five quick-release fasteners (1) anti-clockwise one half turn and remove the battery compartment cover panel (2).

Checking
topping-up
Fig. 1 The vehicle must be on level ground when the electrolyte is being checked.

DO NOT USE A NAKED LIGHT WHEN CHECKING THE LEVELS and do not use tap water for topping-up.

Remove the battery vent cover; use the grip at the centre of the cover (3), this will ensure that the filling valves are operated correctly. If no electrolyte is visible inside the battery, pour distilled or deionised water into the filling trough until the three tubes (4), and the connecting trough (5), are filled. Refit the vent cover. Check the second battery.

The above operations should not be carried out within half an hour of the battery having been charged, other than by the vehicle's own generating system, lest it floods. In extremely cold conditions run the engine immediately after topping-up so as to mix the electrolyte.

Fig. 1

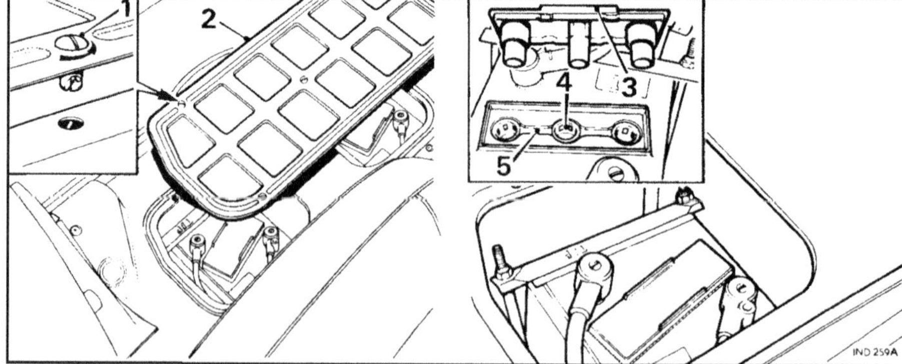

IMPORTANT.–The vent cover must be kept closed at all times, except when topping-up. The electrolyte will flood if the cover is removed for long periods during or within thirty minutes of the battery being normal (5 amp.), or fast charged (30-40 amps.). Single-cell discharge testers cannot be used on these batteries. Operation of the filling device will be destroyed if the battery case is drilled or punctured.

General maintenance
The batteries must be kept dry and clean; cable and battery terminals should be smeared with petroleum jelly.

Do not leave the battery in a discharged state for any length of time. When not in regular use have the battery fully charged, and every four weeks give a short refresher trickle charge to prevent permanent damage to the battery plates.

Specific gravity
The specific gravity of the electrolyte in each cell should be tested at the intervals given in the 'ROUTINE MAINTENANCE SUMMARY' and adjusted as necessary. This should be undertaken by your Distributor or Dealer.

BATTERY BOOSTING AND CHARGING

CAUTION: The following precautions must be observed to avoid the possibility of serious damage to the charging system or electrical components of the vehicle.

Battery boosting
Fig. 2
When connecting an additional battery to boost a discharged battery in the vehicle, ensure that:

- the booster battery is of the same nominal voltage as the vehicle battery;
- the interconnecting cables are of sufficient capacity to carry starting current;
- **the cables are interconnected one at a time and to the booster battery first;**
- the cables are connected between the battery terminals in the following order: first, **+** (positive) to **+** (positive) and then **–** (negative) to **–** (negative);
- the engine speed is reduced to 1,000 rev/min or below before disconnecting the boost battery. The vehicle battery must never be disconnected while the engine is running.

Fig. 2

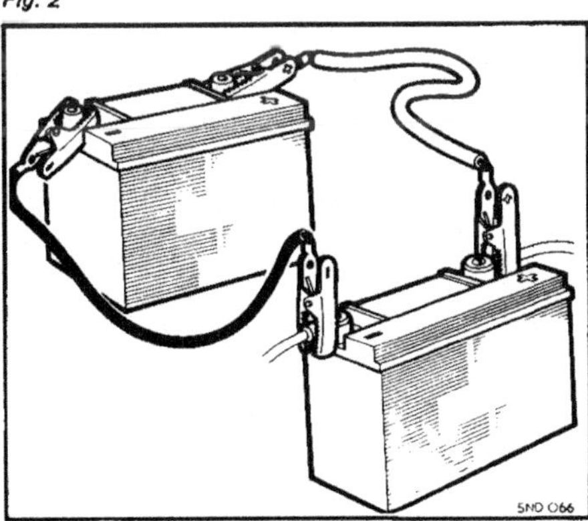

Battery charging When charging the battery in the vehicle from an outside source such as a trickle charger, ensure that:

— the charger voltage is the same as the nominal voltage of the battery;

— the charger positive (+) lead is connected to the positive (+) terminal of the battery;

— the charger negative (−) lead is connected to the negative (−) terminal of the battery.

FUSES

Fig. 3 The fuses are housed under the fuse cover (1) mounted in the engine compartment adjacent to the oil filter.

Fuse connecting 1-2. The fuse (2) protects one parking lamp, one tail lamp, and one number-plate lamp.

Fuse connecting 3-4. The fuse (3) protects one parking lamp, one tail lamp, and one number-plate lamp.

Fuse connecting 5-6. The fuse (4) protects the circuits which operate only when the ignition is switched on. These circuits are for the cooling fans, direction indicators, brake stop lamps, reverse lamps, temperature and fuel gauges, and the heated rear window.

Fuse connecting 7-8. The fuse (5) protects the circuits which operate independently of the ignition switch, namely horns, interior and luggage compartment lamps, headlamp flasher, and the cigar lighter.

Line fuses Fig. 3 **Auxiliary equipment.** The 35 amp. line fuse (7) protects the windscreen wiper, windscreen washer, heater blower motor, and radio circuits when the ignition steering lock key is in position 'I'.

Hazard warning. The 35-amp. line fuse (8) protects the hazard warning lamps and is located behind the hazard warning switch. It is accessible only when the centre console is withdrawn (see page 43).

Radio. A separate additional line fuse protects the radio (if fitted). See the instructions supplied with the radio for the correct fuse ratings.

To change a line fuse, hold one end of the cylindrical fuse holder (9), push in and twist the other end (10). Remove the fuse (11) from the cylindrical holder.

Spare fuses
Fig. 3
Two spare fuses (6) are provided and it is important to use the correct replacement fuse. The fusing value, current rated 17 amp. (35 amp. blow rated), is marked on a coloured slip of paper inside the glass tube of the fuse.

Blown fuses
A blown fuse is indicated by the failure of all the units protected by it, and is confirmed by examination of the fuse when withdrawn. Before renewing a blown fuse inspect the wiring of the units that have failed for evidence of a short-circuit or other fault.

Accessories
Fig. 3
If an electrical accessory is being fitted and it is required to operate independently of the ignition circuit it should be connected to terminal '8' on the fuse block; if it is required to operate only when the ignition is switched on, connect it to terminal '6'. The terminal numbers are marked on the fuse block.

Fig. 3

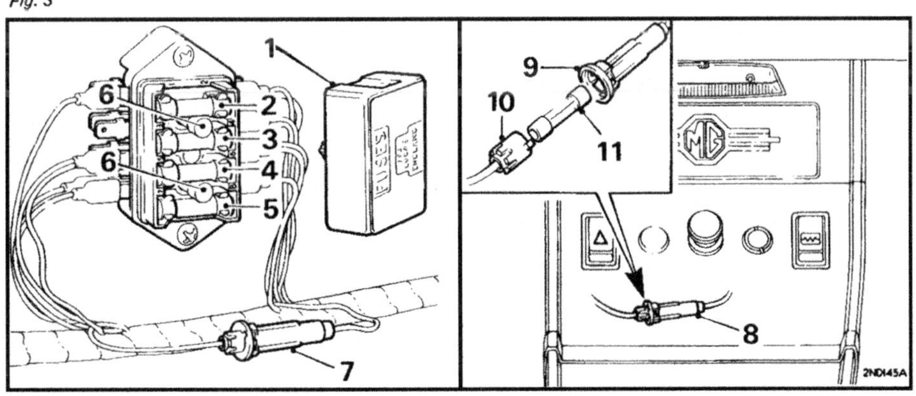

HEADLAMPS

Light unit
Fig. 4

Removing. Ease the bottom of the outer rim (1) forwards away from the lamp. Unscrew the three inner rim retaining screws (2), remove the inner rim (3) withdraw the light unit (4), and disconnect the three-pin plug (5).

Refitting. Connect the three-pin plug and position the light unit in the headlamp body ensuring that the three lugs formed on the outer edge of the light unit engage in the slots formed in the body, and fit the inner retaining rim. Position the outer rim on the retaining lugs with the cut-away portion of the rim at the bottom of the lamp, press the rim downwards and inwards.

Beam setting

Two adjusting screws are provided on each headlamp for setting the main beams. The screw (6) is for adjusting the beam in the vertical plane, and the screw (7) is for horizontal adjustment. The beams must be set in accordance with local regulations; resetting and checking should be entrusted to your Distributor or Dealer, who will have special equipment available for this purpose.

LAMPS

Side and
direction
indicator
Fig. 4

To gain access to the sidelamp (8) and direction indicator (9) bulbs, unscrew the two retaining screws (10) and withdraw the rim and lens.

The bulbs have a bayonet-type fixing.

Fig. 4

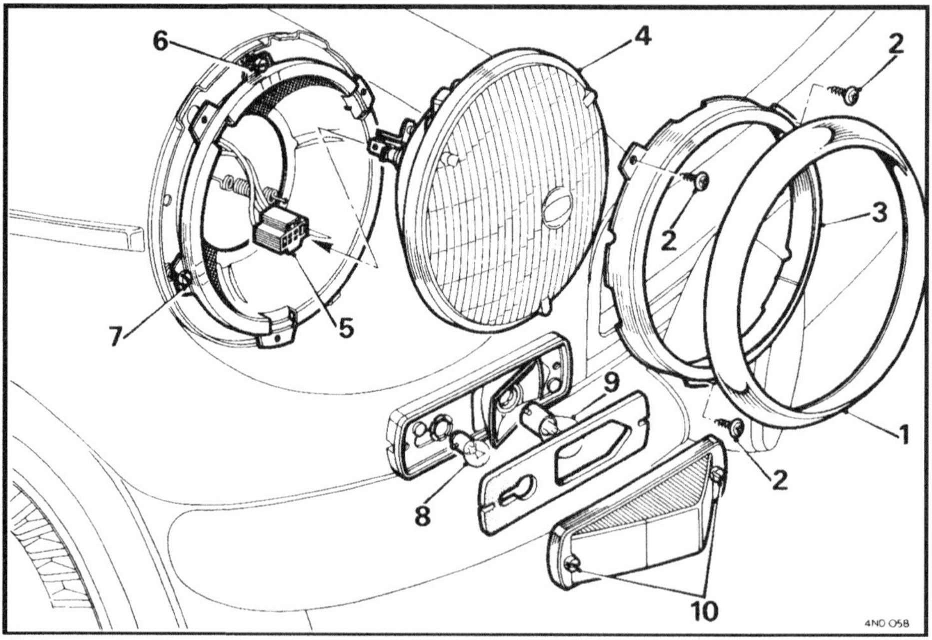

<table>
<tr><td>Stop, tail
and direction
indicator
Fig. 5</td><td>Remove the lens retaining screws (1) and slide the lens upwards to gain access to the direction indicator (2) and stop/tail (3) bulbs.

The direction indicator lamps have a single-filament bulb (2) which may be fitted either way round in the socket. The tail and stop lamp bulb (3) has a twin filament and offset peg bayonet fixing to ensure correct fitment.</td></tr>
<tr><td>Reverse
Fig. 6</td><td>To renew a bulb, remove the two securing screws (1) and withdraw the lens. Press the bulb (2) down towards the lower contact and withdraw it from the lamp.

Fit one end of the new bulb into the hole in the lower contact, then press the top of the bulb into the lamp until the point of the cap engages the hole in the upper contact.</td></tr>
<tr><td>Number-plate
Fig. 7</td><td>To change a bulb, remove the two screws and nuts, remove the lamp hood (1) and lift off the lens (2). When refitting the lens on later cars check that the lens is pushed into the gasket (3). Ensure that the wedge shaped gasket (3) on later cars, or the wedge shaped distance piece (4) on early cars, is fitted with its thickest edge towards the rear.</td></tr>
</table>

Fig. 5

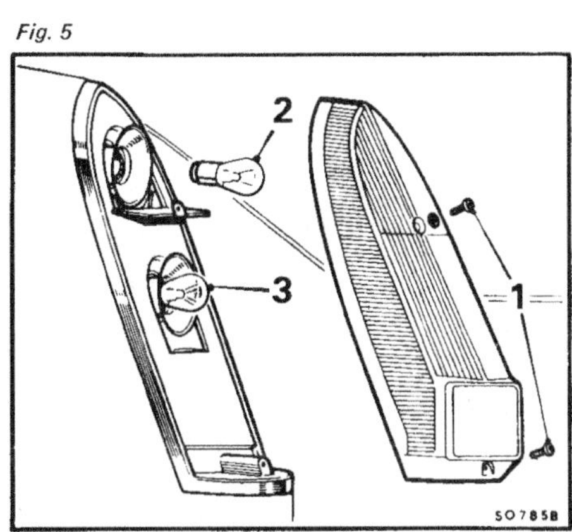

Fig. 6

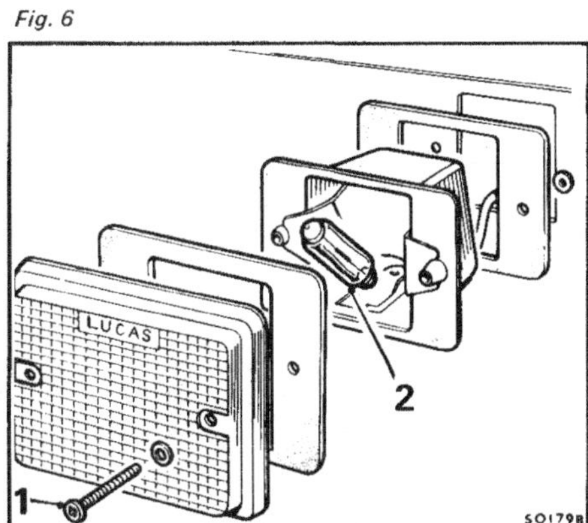

Fig 7

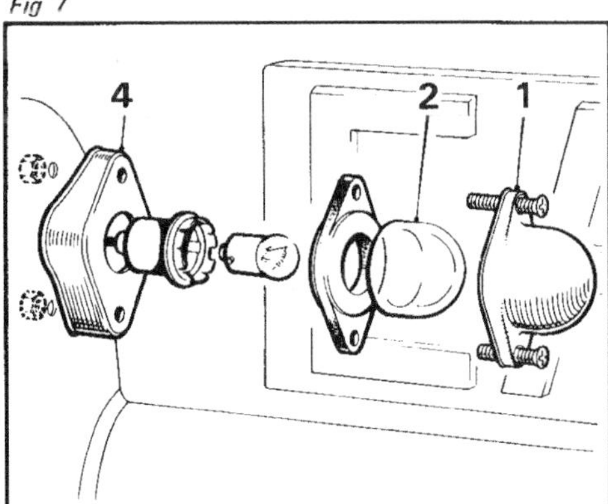

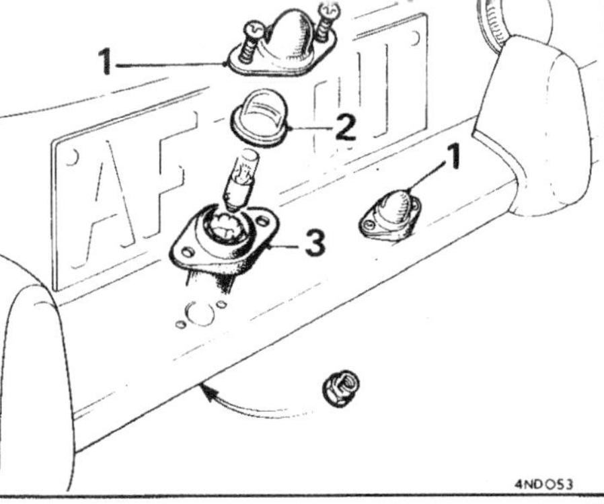

Courtesy To renew a bulb, remove the screws (1) retaining the lamp bezel and remove the
Fig. 8 bezel and lens. The bulb may then be withdrawn from its contacts.

Interior The lens in the lamp is held in position by four locating lugs. To gain access to the
Fig. 9 bulb, gently squeeze the lens sides and pull outwards. Remove the bulb from the
retaining clips.

Panel and The warning and panel lamp holders are a push fit into the back of the instrument
warning lamps and the warning lamps and are located in the positions shown.
Fig. 10

The lamps are accessible from below the fascia panel.

Instrument panel lamp bulbs. A 2.2-watt screw fixing bulb. Remove the push-fit
bulb holders (1) from the instruments and unscrew the bulb (2).

Warning lamp bulbs. A 2-watt miniature bayonet fixing bulb. Remove the push-fit
bulb holders (3) from the lamps and remove the bulbs (4).

Fig. 8

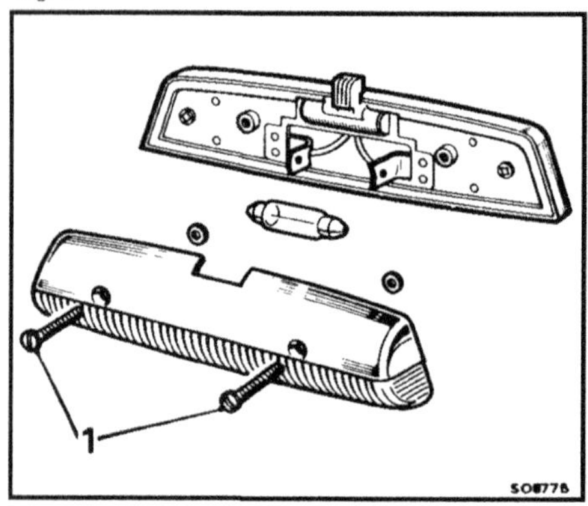

Fig. 9

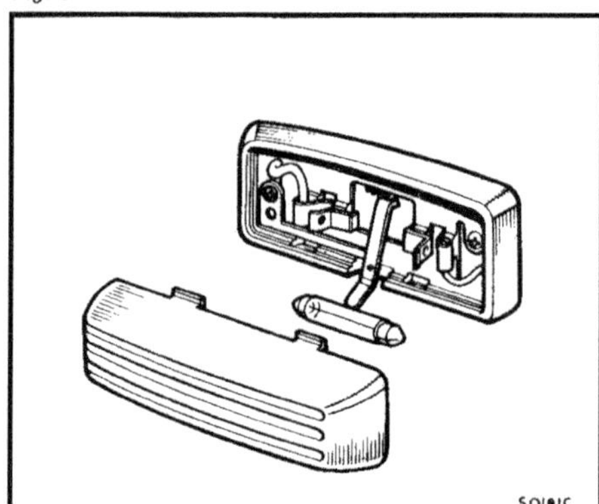

Fig. 10

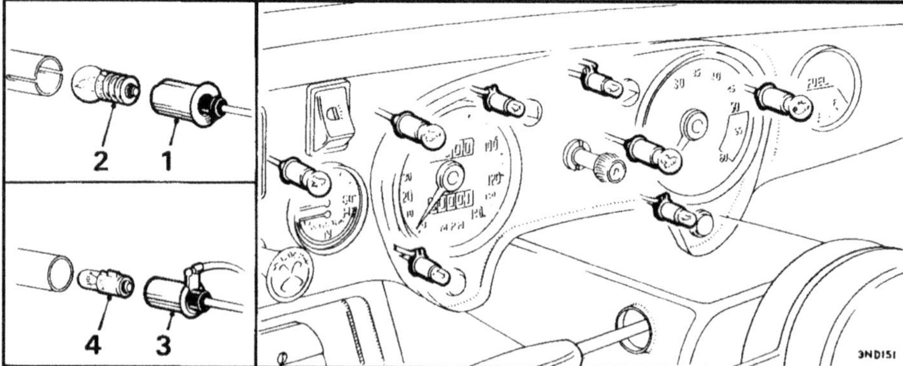

To gain access to the bulbs the centre console must be withdrawn.

Centre console. Remove the gear lever knob and locknut (1). Unscrew the four screws (2) securing the gaiter retaining ring. Raise the hinged arm-rest, unscrew the retaining screw (3) and remove the arm-rest complete with gaiter (4). Unscrew the four screws (5) retaining the console and withdraw the console (6) rearwards.

Heated rear window warning lamp. A 2.2-watt screw fixing bulb. Withdraw the centre console. Remove the push-fit bulb holder (7) from the lamp and unscrew the bulb (8).

Cigar-lighter illumination bulb. A 2.2-watt bulb with bayonet fixing. Withdraw the centre console. Squeeze the sides of the bulb hood (9) and remove the hood. Remove the bulb holder (10) from the hood clip and remove the bulb (11).

Fig. 11

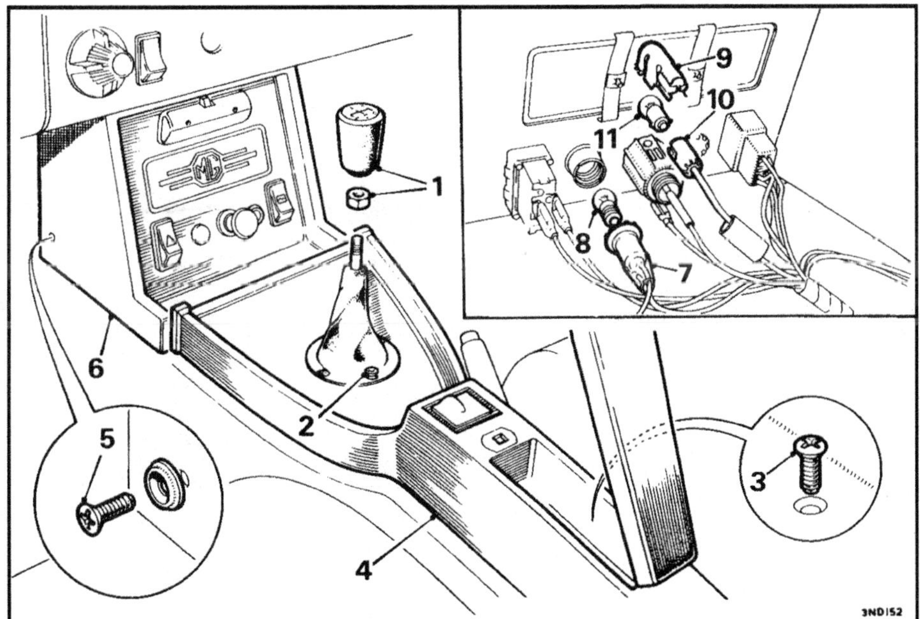

		Volts	*Watts*	*Part No.*
Replacement bulbs	Side lamps	12	5	GLB 989
	Tail and stop lamps	12	5/21	GLB 380
	Reverse lamps	12	18	BFS 272
	Direction indicators	12	21	GLB 382
	Warning lamps–fascia	12	2	GLB 281
	Warning lamp–heated rear window ..	12	2.2	GLB 987
	Instrument illumination	12	2.2	GLB 987
	Cigar-lighter illumination	12	2.2	BFS 643
	Courtesy lamp	12	6	GLB 254
	Interior lamp	12	6	GLB 254
	Number-plate lamps: Early cars	12	5	GLB 207
	Later cars	12	4	BFS 233
Sealed beam unit	Headlamps	12	75/50	GLU 106

WINDSCREEN WIPER AND WASHER

Wiper arms
Fig. 12

To re-position a wiper arm on the spindle, hold the spring clip (1) clear of the retaining groove in the spindle and withdraw the arm. Replace the arm in the required position and push it down onto the spindle (2) until it is secured in position by the retaining clip.

Wiper blade
Fig. 12

To renew a wiper blade pull the arm away from the windscreen. Hold the fastener (3) and the spring retainer (4) away from the wiper arm (5) and withdraw the blade assembly from the arm.

Insert the end of the wiper arm into the spring fastener of the new blade and push the blade into engagement (6) with the arm.

To ensure efficient wiping it is recommended that wiper blades are renewed annually.

Fig. 12

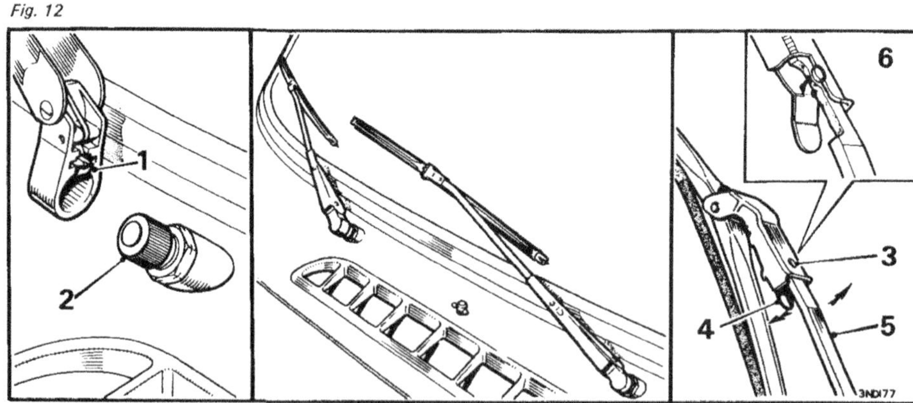

| **Windscreen washer** **Fig. 13** | The windscreen washer system should be checked for correct operation and the reservoir refilled if necessary every week and before a long journey in addition to the mileage intervals given in 'ROUTINE MAINTENANCE SUMMARY'. |

Washer reservoir. To fill the reservoir, remove the cap (1) and lift the reservoir (2) from its mounting.

The reservoir should be filled with a mixture of water and **UNIPART Screenwash** in the recommended proportions to improve visibility in adverse weather conditions. In freezing conditions use **UNIPART 'Four Seasons' Screen Wash.**

On no account should radiator anti-freeze or methylated spirits (denatured alcohol) be used in the windscreen washer.

Jet adjusting. Turn the jet (3) using a small screwdriver to adjust the height of the spray. The spray should strike the top of the windscreen.

ALTERNATOR

The following precautions must be observed to prevent inadvertent damage to the alternator and its control equipment.

Polarity. Ensure that the correct battery polarity is maintained at all times; reversed battery or charger connections will damage the alternator rectifiers.

Battery connections. The battery must never be disconnected while the engine is running.

Testing semi-conductor devices. Never use an ohmmeter of the type incorporating a hand driven generator for checking the rectifiers or the transistors.

STARTER

The starter motor is mounted on the right-hand side of the engine on the flywheel housing. It requires no lubrication.

FUEL PUMP

Fuel is delivered to the carburetters by an S.U. electric fuel pump. The pump is situated beneath the luggage compartment on the right-hand side.

Fig. 13

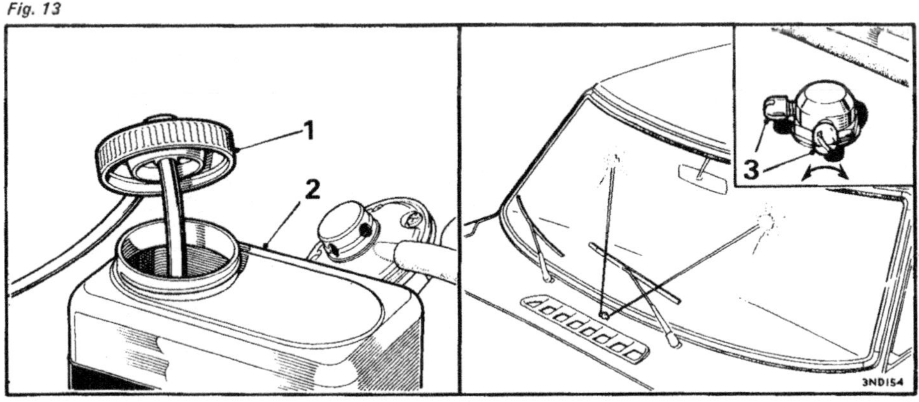

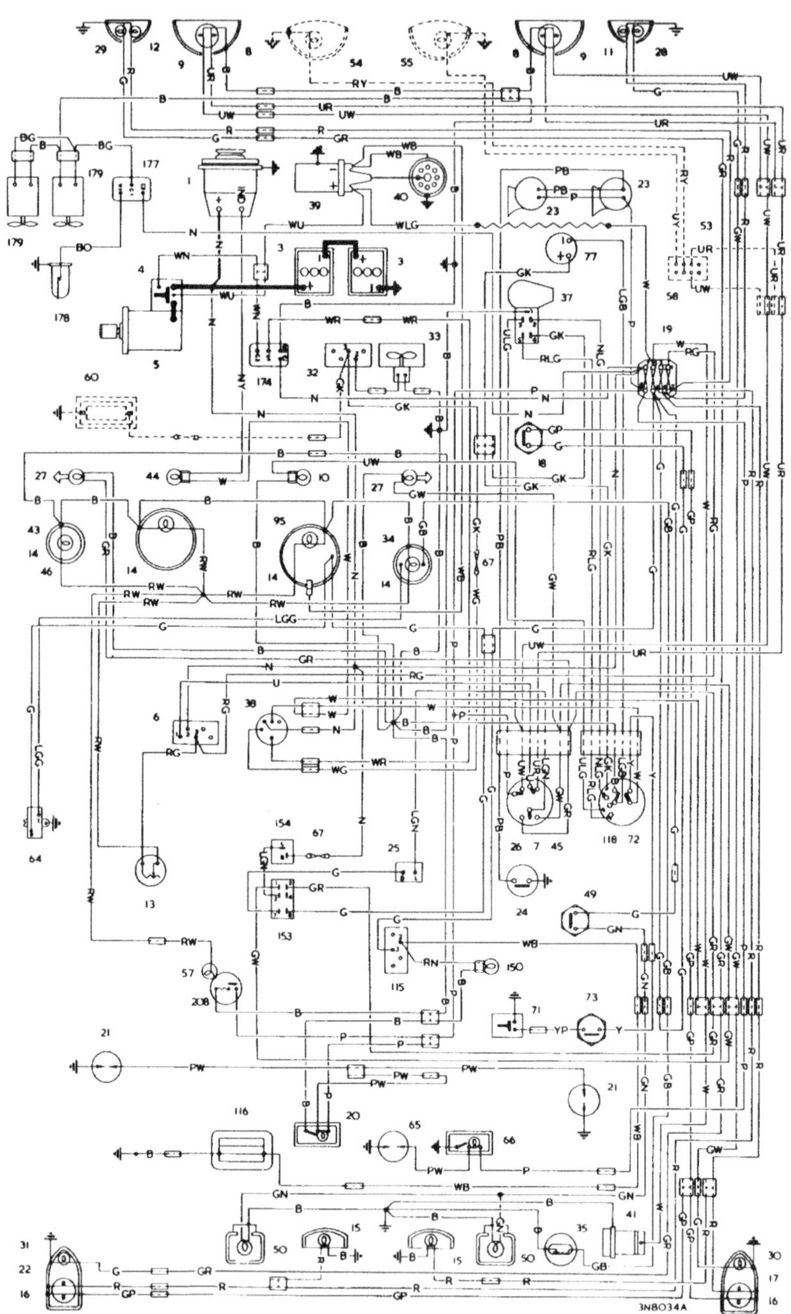
3NB034A

1. Alternator.
3. Batteries (6-volt)/battery (12-volt).
4. Starter solenoid.
5. Starter motor.
6. Lighting switch.
7. Headlamp dip switch.
8. Headlamp dip beam.
9. Headlamp high beam.
10. High-beam warning lamp.
11. R.H. side lamp.
12. L.H. side lamp.
13. Panel lamp rheostat switch.
14. Panel illumination lamps.
15. Number-plate illumination lamps.
16. Stop lamps.
17. R.H. tail lamp.
18. Stop lamp switch.
19. Fuse unit (4-way).
20. Interior lamp.
21. Interior lamp door switches.
22. L.H. tail lamp.
23. Horns.
24. Horn-push.
25. Flasher unit.
26. Direction indicator switch.
27. Direction indicator warning lamps.
28. R.H. front direction indicator lamp.
29. L.H. front direction indicator lamp.
30. R.H. rear direction indicator lamp.
31. L.H. rear direction indicator lamp.
32. Heater motor switch.
33. Heater motor.
34. Fuel gauge.
35. Fuel gauge tank unit.
37. Windscreen wiper motor.
38. Ignition/starter switch.

39. Ignition coil.
40. Distributor.
41. Fuel pump.
43. Oil pressure gauge.
44. Ignition warning lamp.
45. Headlamp flasher switch.
46. Coolant temperature gauge.
49. Reverse lamp switch.
50. Reverse lamp.
53. Fog lamp switch.*
54. Fog lamp.*
55. Driving lamp.*
57. Cigar-lighter illumination bulb.
58. Driving lamp switch.*
60. Radio.*
64. Instrument voltage stabiliser.
65. Luggage compartment lamp switch.
66. Luggage compartment lamp.
67. Line fuse.
71. Overdrive solenoid.
72. Overdrive manual control switch.
73. Overdrive gear switch.
77. Windscreen washer pump.
95. Tachometer.
115. Heated back-light switch.
116. Heated back-light.
118. Combined windscreen washer and wiper switch.
150. Heated back-light warning lamp.
153. Hazard warning switch.
154. Hazard warning flasher unit.
174. Starter solenoid relay.
177. Radiator cooling fan relay.
178. Radiator cooling fan thermostat.
179. Radiator cooling fan motor.
208. Cigar-lighter.

* Optional fitment circuits shown dotted.

CABLE COLOUR CODE

N. Brown	P. Purple	Y. Yellow
U. Blue	G. Green	B. Black
R. Red	L.G. Light Green	K. Pink
	W. White	

When a cable has two colour code letters the first denotes
the main colour and the second denotes the tracer colour.

IGNITION TIMING

The ignition timing is set dynamically to give optimum engine performance with efficient engine emission control. Electronic test equipment must be used to check the ignition timing setting and the automatic advance (see **'GENERAL DATA'**). Checking and adjustment to the ignition timing setting should be carried out by your Distributor or Dealer.

The ignition timing must be checked after cleaning, re-setting, or renewing of the distributor contacts.

DISTRIBUTOR

Fig. 1 Release the retaining clips (1), remove the distributor cap (2) and place to one side. Remove the rotor arm (3).

Cleaning contacts Fig. 2 Inspect the contact points (1) and, if burned, clean with fine emery cloth or fine carborundum stone. Wipe the contacts clean with a fuel-moistened cloth. Renew pitted or worn points.

Lubrication Fig. 2 Remove the moving contact, lightly smear the pivot post (2) and around the cam (3) with grease.

Add a few drops of oil through the hole (4) in the base plate to lubricate the centrifugal weights.

Add a few drops of oil to the felt pad (5) in the top of the cam spindle. Do not remove the felt pad or the screw beneath the felt pad as clearance is provided for oil to pass onto the cam bearings.

Carefully wipe away all surplus lubricant and see that the contact breaker points are perfectly clean and dry.

Fig. 1

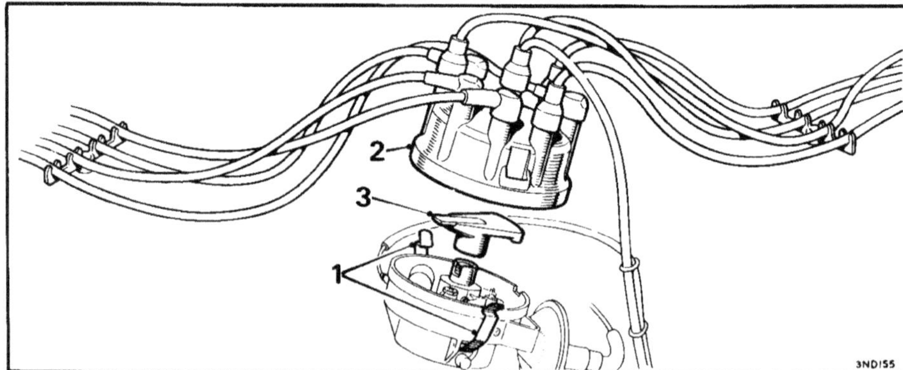

Contact gap
Fig. 2

The contact points must be adjusted by setting the dwell angle (see 'GENERAL DATA') using electronic test equipment. This work should be entrusted to your Distributor or Dealer.

Should it become necessary to change the contact points, and electronic equipment is not available, the contact points may be adjusted as follows:

1. Turn the crankshaft until the points are fully open.
2. Check the contact gap (1) with a feeler gauge (see 'GENERAL DATA'); the gauge should be a sliding fit.
3. If the gap varies appreciably from the gauge thickness turn the adjusting nut (6) clockwise to increase or anti-clockwise to decrease the gap.
4. Refit the rotor, engaging its drive lug in the spindle slot and push the rotor onto the spindle shaft.
5. Wipe the inside of the distributor cap clean and refit it.

IMPORTANT. At the first opportunity the contact points must be checked and adjusted to the dwell angle (see 'GENERAL DATA') by your Distributor or Dealer who will have the necessary electronic equipment.

Contact set
renewing
Fig. 2

Removing. Unscrew the nut (7), lift off the insulating bush (8) and both leads from the stud. Remove the securing screw (9) with its spring washer, and lift off the one-piece contact set. If removal of the moving contact only is required, leave the securing screw (9) in position.

Fitting. Before fitting a new contact set, wipe the points clean with fuel or methylated spirits.

Lubricate the pivot post (2) with grease and check that the insulating bush is correctly positioned (10) below the spring loop. Position the contact set on the base plate, ensuring that the advance pivot pin (11) engages the hole in the vacuum unit linkage (12), and the contact set is seated flat on the base plate. Fit and tighten the securing screw (9). Locate the lead terminals round the insulating bush so that they make contact with the spring and tighten the nut (7).

Fig. 2

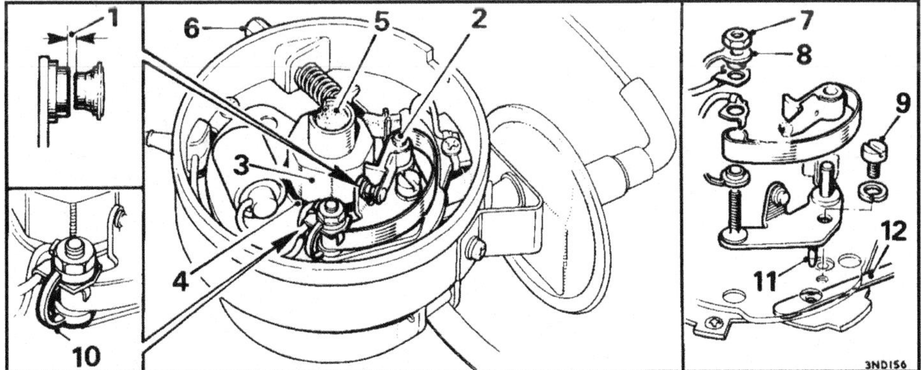

Adjust the contact gap by setting the dwell angle; this work should be entrusted to your Distributor or Dealer.

When a new contact set has been fitted have the gap re-checked by your Distributor or Dealer (who will have the necessary electronic equipment) after the first 500 miles (800 km.). During this period the heel of the contact will have bedded in and reduced the gap.

SPARKING PLUGS

Removing plugs
Fig. 3

Slacken the retaining clamp screw (1) and withdraw the air temperature control (2) from the air cleaner. Remove the two bolts (3) to release the top half of the hot air shroud (4) from the front of each exhaust manifold.

Disconnect the H.T. cables (5) from the sparking plugs. Unscrew the sparking plugs using a **UNIPART Sleevlok Plug Spanner.**

Cleaning and resetting
Fig. 3

The sparking plugs should be cleaned with an air-blast service unit.

Check the plug gaps and reset if necessary to the recommended gap (see **'GENERAL DATA').** To reset, use a special Champion sparking plug gauge and setting tool (7); move the side electrode, never the centre one.

Fig. 3

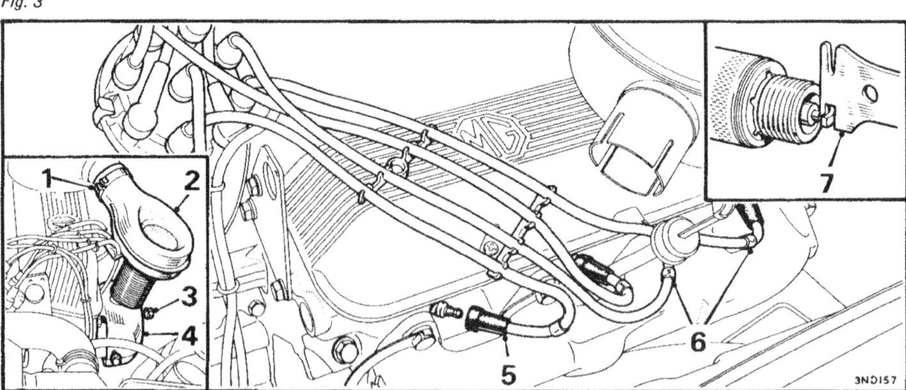

Refitting plugs   Before refitting the plugs ensure that the washers are not defective in any way.

CAUTION: Owing to the angle at which the sparking plugs are fitted it is essential that care is taken when refitting to avoid damage to the threads.

Screw down the plug by hand as far as possible and then use **a UNIPART Sleevlok Plug Spanner** to avoid possible damage to the insulator. Never overtighten a plug but ensure a good joint is made between the plug body, washer and cylinder head. Wipe the plugs clean before reconnecting the H.T. cable.

When fitting new sparking plugs ensure that only the recommended type is used and that they are set to the correct gap before installation (see **'GENERAL DATA'**).

IGNITION CABLES

Positioning   It is essential that the ignition cables to the sparking plugs in the left-hand cylin-
Fig. 3   der head are correctly positioned.

In particular the ignition cables (6) to number five and number seven sparking plugs must be clipped in the position shown and not adjacent to each other.

LUBRICATION

Checking oil level
Fig. 1

Ensure that the vehicle is standing on level ground. The level of the oil in the engine sump is indicated by the dipstick (1) located in the left hand side of the engine. Maintain the level between the 'HIGH' mark (2) and the 'LOW' mark (3) on the dipstick and never allow it to fall below the 'LOW mark.

The oil level should always be checked before a long journey.

The oil filler is on the forward side of the right-hand rocker cover. Unscrew the filler cap (4) by turning it anti-clockwise.

Draining
Fig. 1

The oil should be drained when the engine is warm; remove the drain plug (5) located on the left-hand side at the rear of the sump.

Clean the drain plug; check that the sealing washer is in a satisfactory condition and refit the plug.

Filling

Fill with the correct quantity (see **'GENERAL DATA'**) of a recommended lubricant through the engine filler. Run the engine for a short while then allow it to stand for a few minutes before checking the level with the dipstick. The difference between the 'LOW' and 'HIGH' mark on the dipstick is approximately 1½ pints (0.85 litre).

Fig. 1

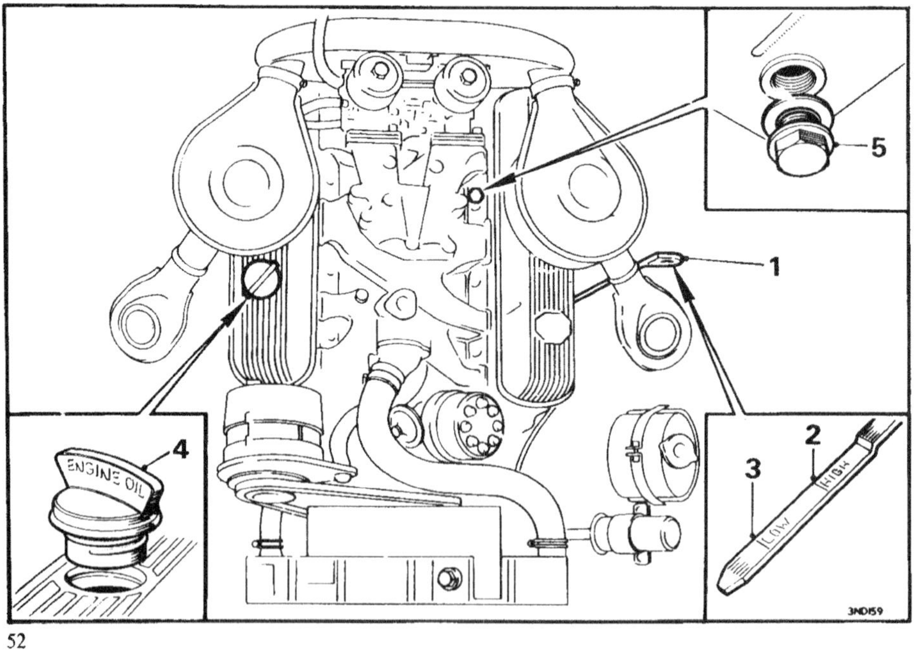

OIL FILTER

Location   The external oil filter is of the disposable cartridge type, and is located on the right-hand front wing valance.

Removing cartridge
Fig. 2   Slacken the cartridge (1) from the filter head.

Hold the union adaptor (2) from turning and unscrew the oil pipe union nut (3) to release the oil pipe from the filter head.

Slacken the three bolts (4) securing the filter head to the mounting bracket.

Unscrew the filter cartridge (1) from the filter head and discard the cartridge. If difficulty is experienced consult your Distributor or Dealer.

Fitting new cartridge
Fig. 2   Smear the new seal (6) with engine oil and fit it into its groove (7) in the new cartridge. Screw the cartridge onto the filter head, using hand force only.

DO NOT USE A SPANNER TO TIGHTEN. DO NOT OVERTIGHTEN.

Tighten the three bolts (4) securing the oil filter head to the mounting bracket.

Hold the adaptor union (2) from turning, and fit and tighten the oil cooler pipe (3).

Check the oil filter for leakage immediately the engine is started.

Fig. 2

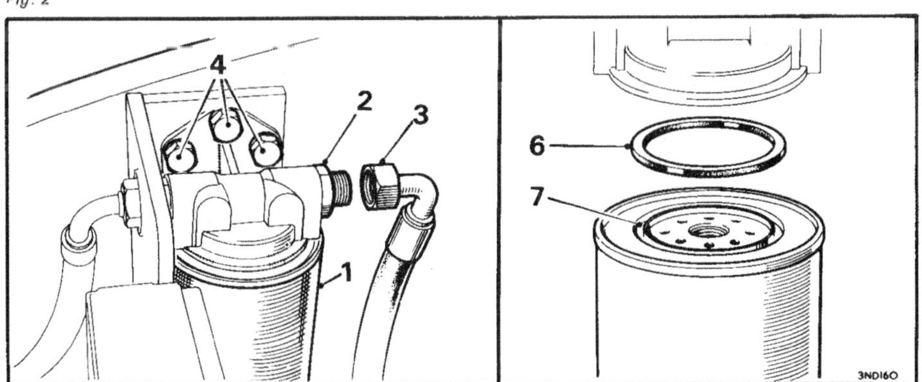

CRANKCASE EMISSION CONTROL

The engine breather outlets on the rocker covers are connected by hoses to the controlled depression chamber between the piston and the throttle disc valve of the carburetters. Oil separator/flame traps are fitted in the hoses. Piston blowby fumes are drawn into the chamber where they combine with the engine inlet charge for combustion in the engine cylinders in the normal way. Fresh filtered air is supplied to the engine crankcase through a hose connected to a filter located behind the air cleaner air-box.

Flame traps
Fig. 3 The flame traps (arrowed) on the top of each rocker cover must be renewed every 12,000 miles (20000 km.) or 12 months.

To remove, withdraw the hoses (1) and (2) from each end of the flame trap and discard the flame trap (3).

Fit the hoses to the new flame trap to secure in position.

Breather
filter
Fig. 4 The breather filter must be renewed every 24,000 miles (40000 km.) or 24 months.

Slacken the hose clips and remove the short hose (1) and the long crankcase hose (2) from the filter. Remove the nut securing the filter clip (3) to the air-box. Withdraw the filter (4) from the clip and discard the filter.

Position the filter in the clip with the end marked 'IN' connected to the short hose (1). Refit the clip to the air-box. Fit the hoses and tighten the hose clips.

Fig. 3

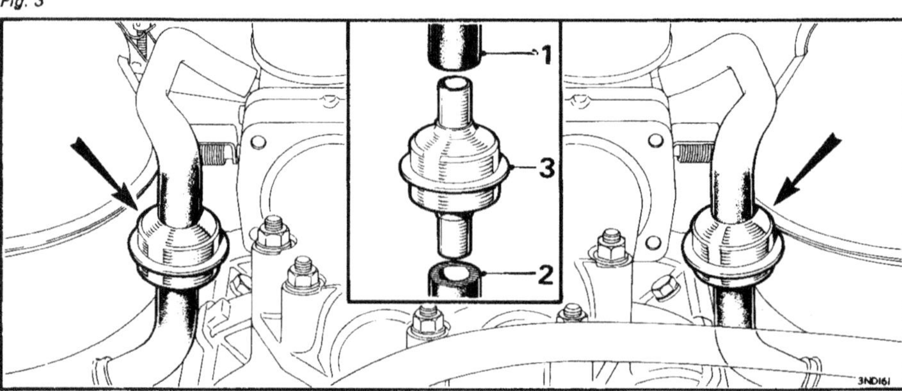

DRIVE BELT

Alternator
Fig. 5

Tension. When correctly tensioned, a total deflection of ½ in. (12 mm.) should be possible at the midway point of the longest belt run between the pulleys.

Adjusting. Slacken the securing bolts (1) and nut and the adjusting link bolts (2). Pivot the alternator upwards to the required position. Apply any leverage necessary to the alternator drive end frame (3) only and not to any other part; to avoid damaging the drive end frame the lever should preferably be of wood or soft metal. Tighten the bolts and re-check the belt tension. **DO NOT OVERTIGHTEN** as this will impose an excess loading on the drive bearings.

Cleaning. Wipe the slip ring end frame (arrowed) clean and check the ventilating apertures are clear.

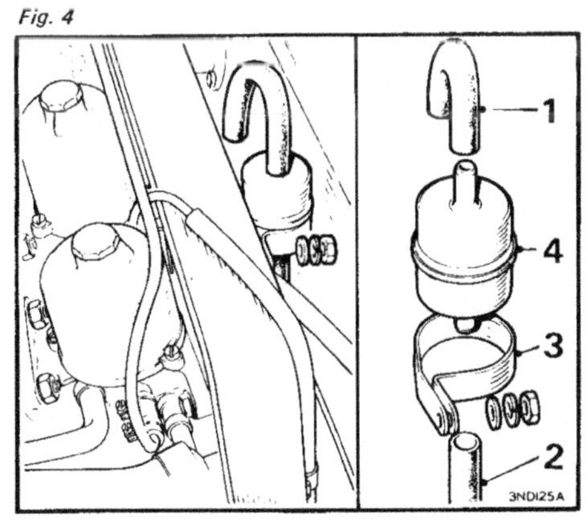

Fig. 4

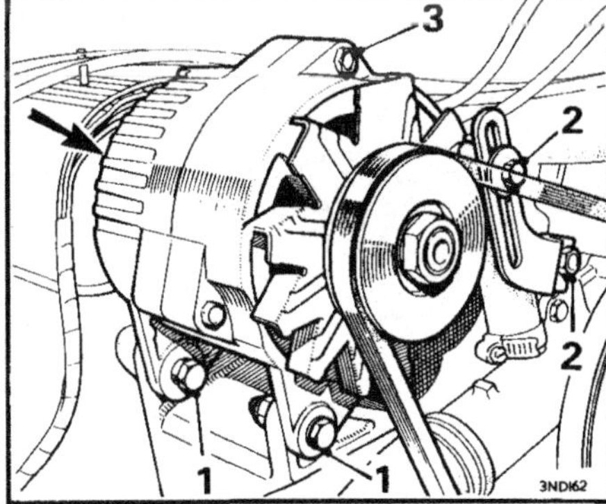

Fig. 5

AIR CLEANERS

The elements of both air cleaners must be renewed every 12,000 miles (20000 km.) or 12 months; more frequent changes may be necessary in dusty operating conditions.

Element changing Fig. 1   Slacken the clamp screw (1) and remove the air temperature control assembly (2) from the air cleaner. Slacken the clamp screw (3) securing the air cleaner to the air-box (early cars only). Unscrew the bolt (4) and remove the air cleaner assembly.

Remove the bolt (4) with its flat washer (5) and sealing grommet (6). Separate the casing, remove the spacer tube (7) and discard the element (8).

Remove the seal (9) from the air cleaner lid and thoroughly clean the air cleaner lid and casing (10). Fit a new element and reassemble ensuring that the seals (6) and (9) are in a satisfactory condition; renew the seals if necessary.

Fig. 1

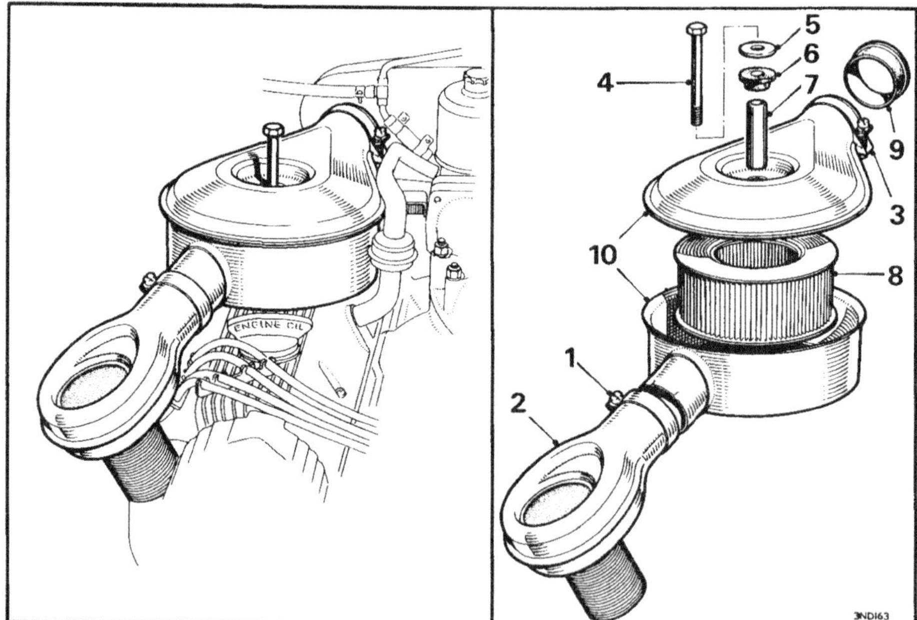

Air temperature control
Fig. 2

Checking. Note the position of the valve plate (arrowed), depress the valve plate and release it. Check to ensure that the valve plate returns to its original position.

If the valve plate does not return to its original position consult your Distributor or Dealer.

FUEL LINE FILTER

The filter must be renewed every 12,000 miles (20000 km.) or 12 months.

Renewing filter
Fig. 3

Slacken the hose clips and remove the fuel tank delivery hose (1) and the carburetter feed hose (2) from the filter (4). Slacken the screw (3) clamping the filter in position. Withdraw the filter from the clip and discard it.

Fit the new filter into the clip with the end marked 'IN' connected to the fuel tank delivery hose (1). Tighten the clamp screw. Fit the hoses and tighten the hose clips.

Fig. 2

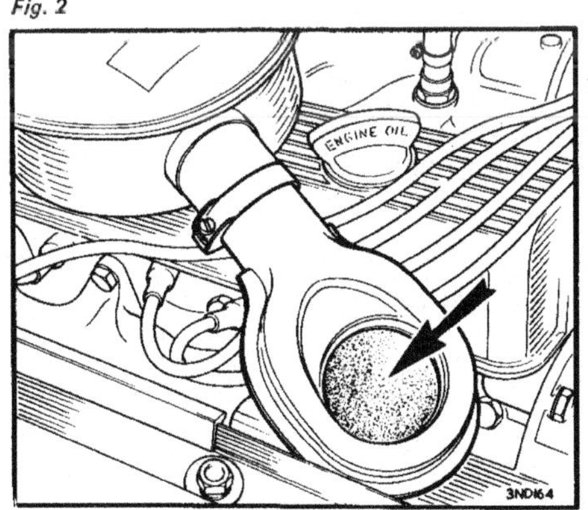

Fig. 3

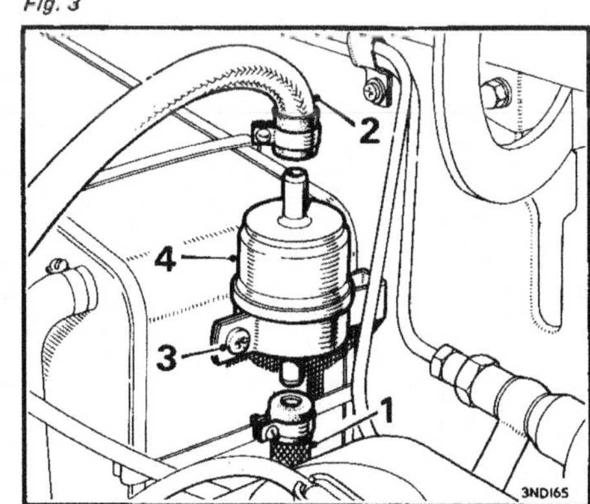

CARBURETTERS

Carburetter damper topping-up
Fig. 5

CAUTION: When lifting the piston and damper, **care must be taken not to dislodge the damper retaining clip** (10) which is pressed into the top of the piston rod. Should the retainer become dislodged, consult your Distributor or Dealer.

Unscrew the cap (11) of each carburetter suction chamber and **gently** lift the piston and damper up to the top of their travel. Fill the retaining recess (12) with oil and push the damper down until the cap contacts the top of the suction chamber. Repeat this filling procedure until the oil level is just visible at the bottom of the retainer recess. Screw the cap firmly into the suction chamber.

Failure to lubricate the piston dampers will cause piston flutter and affect acceleration.

Linkage lubrication

Lubricate the carburetter accelerator and choke linkages and cables and the accelerator pedal pivot.

Carburetter tuning
Figs. 4 and 5

The efficient operation of the engine and any exhaust emission control equipent which may be fitted depends on correct ignition timing, distributor contact breaker and plug gaps. It is essential that these items are checked before adjusting the carburetters.

Carburetter tuning must be confined to setting the idle and fast idle speeds and mixture at idle speed. A reliable tachometer and a carburetter intake balancing meter should be used.

IMPORTANT: Where a vehicle must conform to exhaust emission control regulations, adjustments should only be carried out if a reliable tachometer, balancing meter and exhaust gas analyser (CO meter) are available.

1. Top up the carburetter piston dampers if necessary to the correct level.
2. Check that the throttle functions correctly.
3. Ensure that the mixture control (choke) will return fully, that the cable has $\frac{1}{16}$ in. (2 mm.) free play (1) before it starts to pull on the lever and a small clearance exists between the fast idle screws (13) and the cams.
4. Remove the air cleaner.

Fig. 4

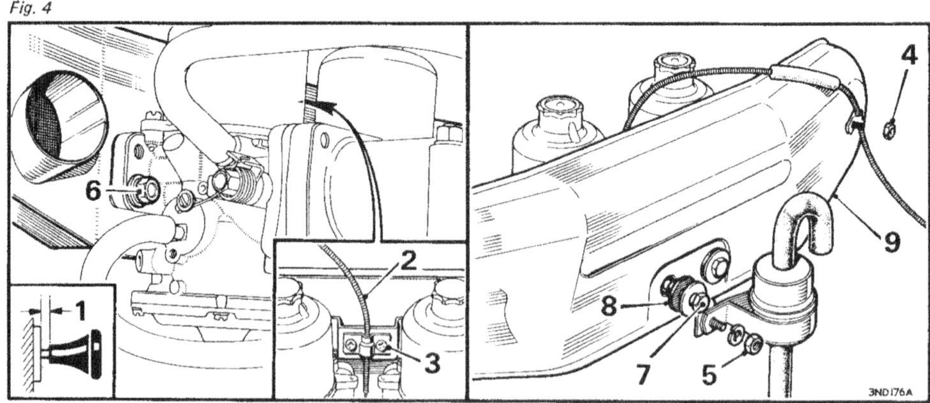

5. Unscrew the two screws (3) to release the mixture control (choke) cable clamp, remove the nut (4) and withdraw the mixture control (choke) cable support clip from the air-box.

6. Remove the nut (5) to release the engine breather filter and its clip from the air-box.

7. Unscrew the air-box securing bolt (6) from each carburetter flange.

8. Unscrew the two bolts (7) with their grommets and spacers (8) and remove the air-box (9).

9. Raise each carburetter piston using the lifting pin (14), release the pin and check that the piston falls freely onto the bridge of the carburetter, indicated by a distinct metallic click. If the piston fails to fall freely, consult your Distributor or Dealer.

10. Connect a tachometer.

    Start the engine and run it at a fast idle speed until it attains normal running temperature, then run it for a further five minutes. Increase the engine speed to 2,500 r.p.m. for 30 seconds.

NOTE.—Tuning can now be commenced. If the adjustment cannot be completed within three minutes, increase the engine speed to 2,500 r.p.m. for 30 seconds and then continue tuning. Repeat this clearing procedure at three-minute intervals until tuning is completed.

Fig. 5

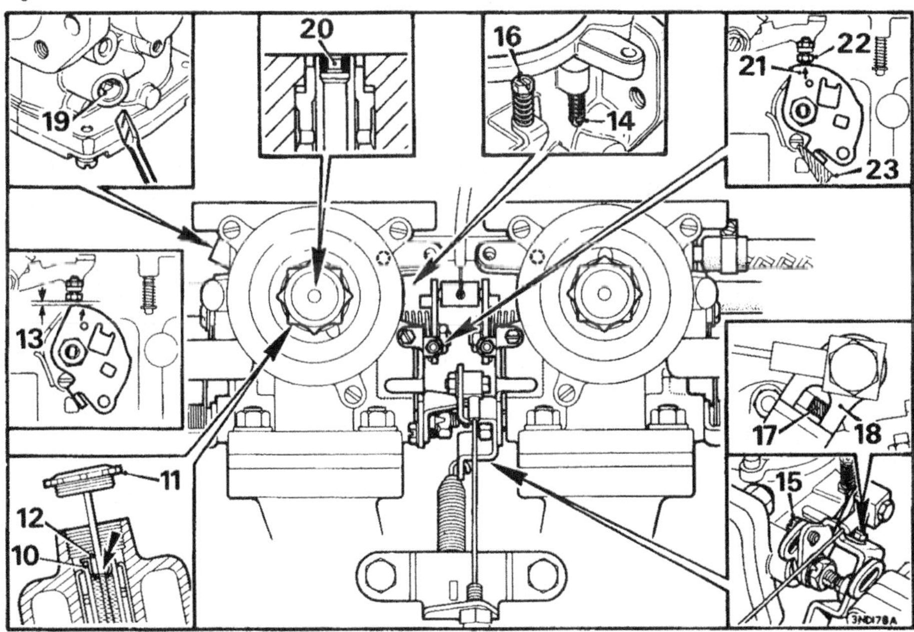

11. Check the idle speed using a tachometer (see 'GENERAL DATA') and check the carburetters for balanced intake using a balance meter.
12. If the balance is not correct adjust as follows: Slacken the lost motion lever adjusting screw (15) and turn the adjusting screw (16) on one of the carburetters until the balance is correct. Turn the throttle adjusting screw (16) on each carburetter by the same amount to adjust the idle speed. Recheck the carburetter balance.
13. Move the arm of the lost motion lever (17) rearwards until it contacts the rear edge of the throttle lever (18) and tighten the screw (15).

If a smooth idle at the correct speed and balance is not obtainable, adjust the idle speed mixture setting as follows:

14. Stop the engine. Remove each suction chamber and piston and screw the jet adjusting screw (19) in until the jets (20) are flush with the bridge of the carburetter or as high as possible without exceeding the height of the bridge. Turn the jet adjusting screw (19) on each carburetter clockwise 2½ turns.
    Refit the piston and suction chambers and top up the piston damper oil levels.
    NOTE.–This operation need not be carried out if it is known that the jets are in the same relative position.
15. Re-start the engine and run it at idle speed.
16. Turn the jet adjusting screw (19) on each carburetter clockwise to enrich or anti-clockwise to weaken, by the same amount until the fastest speed is indicated; turn each screw anti-clockwise until the engine speed just commences to fall. Turn each screw very slowly clockwise by the minimum amount until the maximum speed is regained.
17. Using the exhaust gas analyser, check that the percentage CO reading is within the prescribed limits. If the reading falls outside the limits, reset both jet adjusting screws by the minimum amount necessary to bring the reading just within the limits.
18. Re-check the idle speed and carburetter balance and adjust as necessary by turning the throttle adjusting screws. Stop the engine.
19. Move the mixture control cam until the arrow (21) marked on the cam is positioned under the fast idle adjusting screw (22) of each carburetter. Use a wedge (23) to hold each cam in this position.
20. Start the engine and using the balancing meter to ensure equal adjustment, turn the fast idle adjusting screws to give the correct fast idle speed (see **'GENERAL DATA'**). Stop the engine.
21. Refit the air-box.
22. Secure the choke cable (2) in the clamp plate and tighten the two screws. Check that a ⅟₁₆ in. (2 mm.) free movement (1) exists before the cable moves the cam. To adjust: slacken the two screws and reposition the outer cable in the clamp.
23. Refit the choke cable support clip to the air-box.
24. Refit the engine breather filter and its clip to the air-box.
25. Refit the air cleaners.

STEERING
Front wheel alignment

Incorrect wheel alignment can cause excessive and uneven tyre wear.

Fig. 1 The front wheels must be set so the distance **(A)** is $\frac{1}{16}$ in. (1.6 mm.) to $\frac{3}{32}$ in. (2.4 mm.) (toe in) less than the distance **(B).**

Wheel alignment requires the use of a special gauge and this work should be entrusted to your Distributor or Dealer.

SUSPENSION
Lubrication

Fig. 2 The two lubricating nipples (arrowed) on each of the swivel pins should be charged periodically with one of the recommended greases.

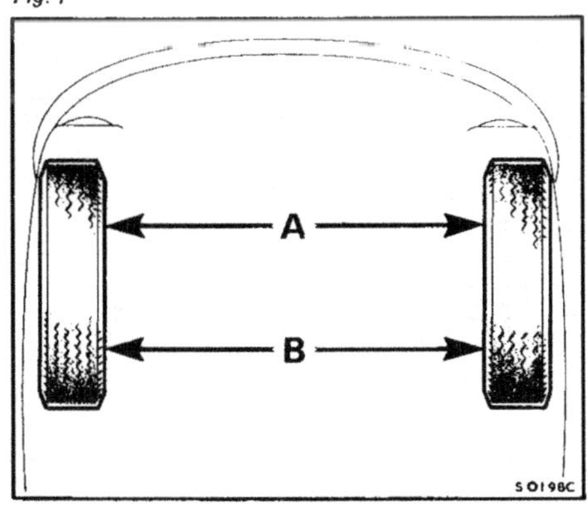

Fig. 1

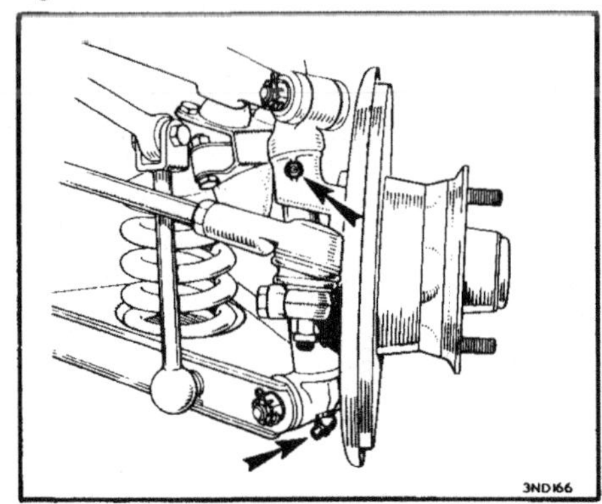

Fig. 2

GEARBOX
Checking
Fig. 1 A combined oil filler and level plug (1) is located on the right-hand side of the gearbox. The oil level must be maintained at the bottom of the plug aperture; ensure that the car is standing level when checking. After topping up the oil level, allow sufficient time for any surplus oil which may have been added to run out of the aperture before replacing the plug.

REAR AXLE
Checking
Fig. 2 A combined oil filler and level plug (1) is located on the rear of the axle. The oil level must be maintained at the bottom of the plug aperture; ensure that the car is standing level when checking. After topping up the oil level, allow sufficient time for any surplus oil which may have been added to run out of the aperture before replacing the plug.

Do not drain the rear axle when the After-Sales Service is carried out.

OVERDRIVE
Maintenance The gearbox and overdrive unit oil must be drained, and the sump filter and the relief valve filter cleaned, every 24,000 miles (40000 km.) or 24 months.

Draining
Fig. 3 To drain the gearbox and overdrive unit, remove the drain plug (1) located on the under-side of the gearbox.

Clean the drain plug and refit.

Sump filter
Fig. 3 Drain the gearbox and overdrive unit. Clean the sump cover and its immediate surroundings.

Remove the cover securing screws (2), withdraw the cover (3) and the filter (4).

Clean all metallic particles from the two magnets (5) fitted to the inside of the cover, wash the cover and the filter in fuel (petrol).

Refit the filter and cover.

Fig. 1

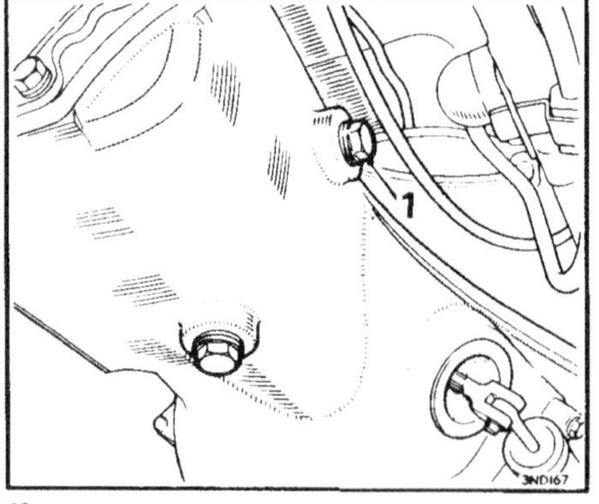

Fig. 2

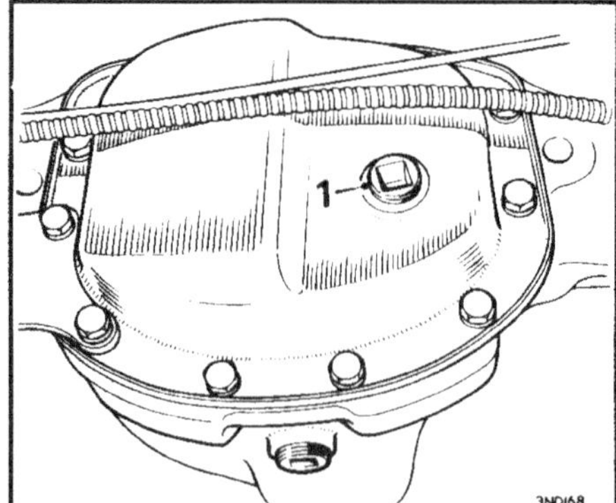

Drain the gearbox and overdrive unit. Clean the relief valve filter plug and its immediate surrounding area.

Remove the relief valve filter plug (6) and the sealing washer (7), withdraw the relief valve (8) and remove the filter (9).

Check that the seal (10) fitted in the plug is in a satisfactory condition.

Wash the filter, plug, sealing washer and seal in fuel (petrol).

Insert the seal (10) into the plug.

Fit the filter to the relief valve, push the valve upwards and refit the plug and sealing washer.

Remove the combined filler and oil level plug (11). Fill the gearbox and overdrive unit with the correct quantity (see **'GENERAL DATA'**) of one of the recommended oils up to the bottom of the plug aperture. Allow sufficient time for any surplus oil to run out before replacing the plug.

Start the engine, and run the car for a short distance, switch off, allow it to stand for a few minutes, then re-check the oil level and top up if necessary.

Fig. 3

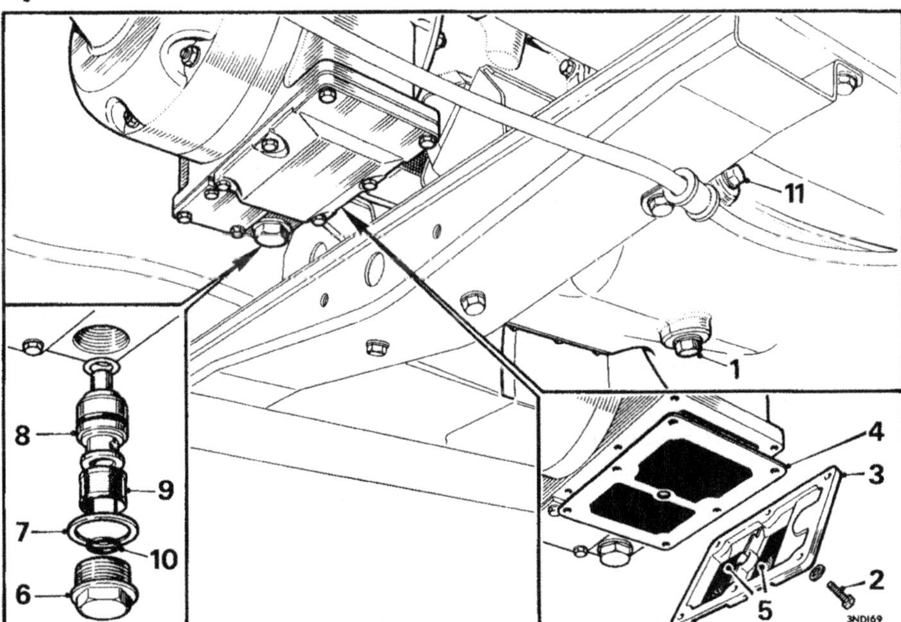

ROUTINE MAINTENANCE SUMMARY

LEYCARE SERVICE

British Leyland Distributors and Dealers operating Leycare Service will, on request, provide a copy of the Leycare Service Job Sheet giving exact details of the work carried out at the prescribed interval and of any further work required. Leycare Service Job Sheets are updated as modifications affecting routine maintenance are introduced and as a result may differ from the Maintenance Summary content published in this Handbook.

Detailed maintenance instructions will be found on the page in brackets after each item.

In addition to the periodic maintenance the following checks should be made weekly:

Check/top up engine oil (52)

Check/top up brake fluid reservoir (34)

Check/top up battery electrolyte (36, 78)

Check/top up cooling system (26)

Check/top up washer reservoir (45)

Check function of original equipment, i.e. exterior lamps, wipers, and warning indicators

Check tyres for tread depth, visually for external cuts in fabric, exposure of ply or cord structure, lumps and bulges.

Check/adjust tyre pressures, including spare (31, 68)

Check tightness of wheel fastenings (29, 68).

MAINTENANCE INTERVALS

Carry out the service indicated by **X** in column:

A at **6,000 mile (10000 km.)** or **6 month** intervals

B at **12,000 mile (20 000 km.)** or **12 month** intervals

Items included in the **3,000 mile (5000 km.)** or **3 month** interval Inspection Check are indicated in column C

ENGINE

	A	B	C
Check/top up engine oil (52)			X
Renew engine oil and filter (52 and 53)	X	X	
Renew carburetter air cleaner elements (56)		X	
Top up carburetter piston dampers (58)	X	X	
Check/adjust carburetter idle speed and mixture settings (58)	X	X	
Renew engine breather filter (54)		24	
Renew engine flame traps (54)		X	
Renew fuel line filter (57)		X	
Check cooling/heater systems for leaks and hoses for security and condition	X	X	
Check/top up cooling system (26)	X	X	X
Check/adjust operation of screen washers and top up reservoir (45)	X	X	X
Check driving belts; adjust or renew (55)	X	X	X
Lubricate accelerator control linkage and pedal pivot – check operation	X	X	

IGNITION

	A	B	C
Clean/adjust sparking plugs (50)	X		
Renew spark plugs (50)		X	
Lubricate distributor (48)	X	X	
Check distributor points; adjust or renew (48)*	X	X	
Check/adjust ignition timing and distributor characteristics using electronic equipment	X	X	

TRANSMISSION

	A	B	C
Check/top up gearbox and rear axle oil (62)	X	X	
Check/top up clutch fluid reservoir (34)	X	X	X
Gearbox with overdrive – drain, clean filters, and fill with new oil (62)		24	

24 = 24,000 miles or 24 months or 40000 km. intervals

	A	B	C
STEERING AND SUSPENSION			
Check for oil/fluid leaks	X	X	X
Check hydraulic dampers for fluid leaks	X	X	X
Check condition and security of steering unit/joints and gaiters	X	X	X
Check/adjust front wheel alignment (61)*	X	X	
Lubricate swivel pins and swivel pin lower links (61)	X	X	
BRAKES			
Check visually hydraulic pipes and unions for chafing, leaks and corrosion	X	X	X
Check/top up brake fluid reservoir (34)	X	X	X
Check/adjust foot brake and hand brake operation to manufacturer's specification (32)	X	X	X
Inspect brake pads for wear and discs for condition (32)*	X		
Inspect brake linings/pads for wear, drums/discs for condition (32)*		X	
Lubricate hand brake mechanical linkage and cables	X	X	
Clean servo filter element (34)		X	
ELECTRICAL			
Check function of original equipment, i.e. interior and exterior lamps, horns, windscreen wiper and warning indicators	X	X	X
Check/top up battery electrolyte (36, 78)	X	X	X
Clean and grease battery connections	X	X	
Check/adjust headlamp alignment (40)*	X	X	X
Check, if necessary renew, windscreen wiper blades (44)	X	X	X
EXHAUST, FUEL AND CLUTCH PIPES			
Check exhaust system for leakage and security	X	X	X
Check visually fuel and clutch pipes and unions for chafing, leaks and corrosion	X	X	X
Check fuel filler pipe/tank connections	X	X	X
WHEELS AND TYRES			
Check that tyres comply with manufacturer's specification (67)	X	X	X
Check tyres for tread depth, visually for cuts in fabric, exposure of ply or cord structure, lumps or bulges	X	X	X
Check/adjust tyre pressures, including spare (31 and 68)	X	X	X
Check tightness of road wheel nuts (29 and 68)	X	X	X
BODY			
Lubricate all locks and hinges (not steering lock) (17)	X	X	
Check condition and security of seats and seat belts (21 and 22)	X	X	X
Check rear view mirror for cracks and crazing	X	X	X
GENERAL			
Road/roller test and check function of all instrumentation	X	X	

* Your Distributor or Dealer should check these items.

NOTE—Take the advice of your Distributor or Dealer on the need for:

1. More frequent oil changes;
2. Additional brake maintenance.

The vehicle specification may vary according to market requirements and from model to model. The Manufacturers reserve the right to alter specifications with or without notice at any time. The policy of constant product improvement by the Manufacturers may involve major or minor changes to the vehicle specification. Whilst every effort is made to ensure accuracy of the particulars contained in this Handbook, no liability for inaccuracies or the consequences thereof can be accepted by the Manufacturer or the Dealer or Distributor who supplied the Handbook.

During running-in from new certain adjustments vary from the specification figures detailed. They will be set to specification by your Dealer or Distributor at the **After Sales Free Service** and should thereafter be maintained throughout the car's life.

Engine	Engine type	V8
	Bore	3.50 in. (88.90 mm.)
	Stroke	2.80 in. (71.12 mm.)
	No. of cylinders	8
	Capacity	215.54 in.^{3}(3532 c.c.)
	Compression ratio	8.26 : 1
	Firing order	1, 8, 4, 3, 6, 5, 7, 2
	Cylinder numbering:	
	Left bank	1, 3, 5, 7
	Right bank	2, 4, 6, 8
	Idle speed	800 to 850 rev/min.
	Fast idle speed	1400 to 1500 rev/min.
	Oil pressure: Normal	30 to 40 lb./in.^{2} (2 to 2.8 kg./cm.^{2})
Ignition	Timing at 1000 rev/min.	8° B.T.D.C.
	Timing marks	On crankshaft pulley pointer attached to front of cylinder block
	Dwell angle	28°
	Contact breaker gap	0.014 to 0.016 in. (0.35 to 0.40 mm.)
	Spark plugs	Champion L–92Y
	Plug gap	0.035 in. (0.90 mm.)
Fuel system	Recommended octane rating ..	94 R O N minimum
	Carburetters	Twin SU type HIF 6
	Needle	BBU
	Spring colour	Yellow
	Fuel pump	SU type AUF 305 electric
Electrical	Circuit polarity	Negative (−) earth
	Voltage	12V
	Batteries	Two 6 volt
	Capacity (20 hour rate)	67 amp.-hour
	Fuses	35 amp. (blow rating)

Transmission	Overdrive ratio	0.82 : 1	
	Gear ratios: First	3.138 : 1	
	Second	1.974 : 1	
	Third	1.259 : 1	**Overdrive**
	Fourth	1 : 1	0.82 : 1
	Reverse	2.819 : 1	
	Final drive ratio	3.071 : 1	
	Overall ratios: First	9.637 : 1	
	Second	6.062 : 1	
	Third	3.866 : 1	
	Fourth	3.071 : 1	2.518 : 1
	Reverse	8.657 : 1	
	Top gear speed per 1000 rev/min. ..	23 m.p.h.	28 m.p.h.
		(37 km.p.h.)	(45 km.p.h.)
Capacities	Fuel tank	12 gallons (54 litres)	
	Engine and oil cooler:		
	Refill with filter change ..	8 pints (4.54 litres)	
	Filter	½ pint (0.28 litres)	
	Gearbox and overdrive	6 pints (3.4 litres)	
	Rear axle	1½ pints (0.85 litres)	
	Cooling system with heater ..	16 pints (9.08 litres)	
	Windscreen washer bottle	3 pints (1.71 litres)	
Dimensions	Overall length	154¾ in. (3.9 m.)	
	Overall width	59 $\frac{15}{16}$ in. (152.3 cm.)	
	Overall height	49 $\frac{31}{32}$ in. (126.9 cm.)	
	Ground clearance; at front of rear		
	silencer—gross car weight ..	4¼ in. (108 mm.) minimum	
	Track: Front	49 in. (124.4 cm.)	
	Rear	49¼ in. (125 cm.)	
	Wheel base	91$\frac{1}{8}$ in. (231.5 cm.)	
Steering	Turning circle:		
	Left lock	34 ft. (10.36 m.)	
	Right lock	33 ft. 1 in. (10.1 m.)	
	Front wheel alignment	$\frac{1}{16}$ in. to $\frac{3}{32}$ in. (1.6 to 2.4 mm.) toe-in	
Wheels and tyres	Wheel size	5J x 14	
	Wheel nut tightness	60 lbf. ft. (8 kgf. m., 81 Nm)	
	Tyres: Size	175HR x 14	
	Type	Radial ply	

General Data

Tyre pressures

Condition	Front				Rear			
	lbf./in.^{2}	kgf/cm^2	kN/m^2	Bars	lbf./in.^{2}	kgf/cm^2	kN/m^2	Bars
Normal car weight	21	1.5	144.79	1.45	25	1.8	172.36	1.72
Gross car weight and sustained speed	26	1.8	179.26	1.79	32	2.25	220.63	2.21

Weights

	Loading conditions	Total weight	Distribution	
			Front	*Rear*
Kerbside	Including full fuel tank and all optional extras.	2442 lb. (1108 kg.)	1207 lb. (548 kg.)	1235 lb. (560 kg.)
Normal	Kerbside weight including driver and passenger	2742 lb. (1244 kg.)	1317 lb. (597 kg.)	1425 lb. (647 kg.)
Gross	Maximum weight condition, refer to note below	2892 lb. (1312 kg.)	1288 lb. (584 kg.)	1604 lb. (728 kg.)
Maximum permissible towing weight		1680 lb. (762 kg.)		
Maximum tow bar hitch load		100 lb. (45 kg.)		
Maximum roof rack load		50 lb. (23 kg.)		

NOTE: Due consideration must be given to the overall weight carried when fully loading the car. Any load carried on the roof rack or downward load from a towing hitch must also be included in the gross car weight.

TUNING MODIFICATIONS

Owners Service Statement   The car as delivered from the factory in its standard form is tuned to give maximum performance with complete reliability, but any super-tuning must inevitably tend to reduce this reliability. For this reason the new car **Owners Service Statement will be invalidated by any form of super-tuning.**

Air pollution, noise, safety regulations   Owners are reminded that in some countries legislation exists covering air pollution, safety or noise limitations on motor vehicles. **Before a car is supertuned or modified,** it is the owner's responsibility to ensure that the proposed alterations and additions are either approved by the appropriate authority for use on the road, or do not contravene the standards set by legislation.

Kits/parts   **Leyland ST Pluspacs** are obtainable from your Leyland ST Distributor/Stockist. Replacement parts and additional parts are designated **Leyland ST Plusparts,** when a replacement is required advise your Dealer that a **Leyland Pluspart** is required

For further details see your Distributor or Dealer or write to:

Leyland ST
Abingdon-on-Thames, Oxfordshire OX14 1AU

SNA 004 B

Fig. 1

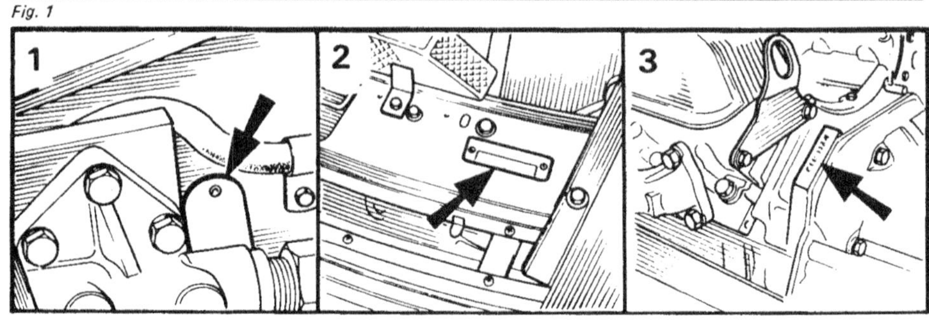

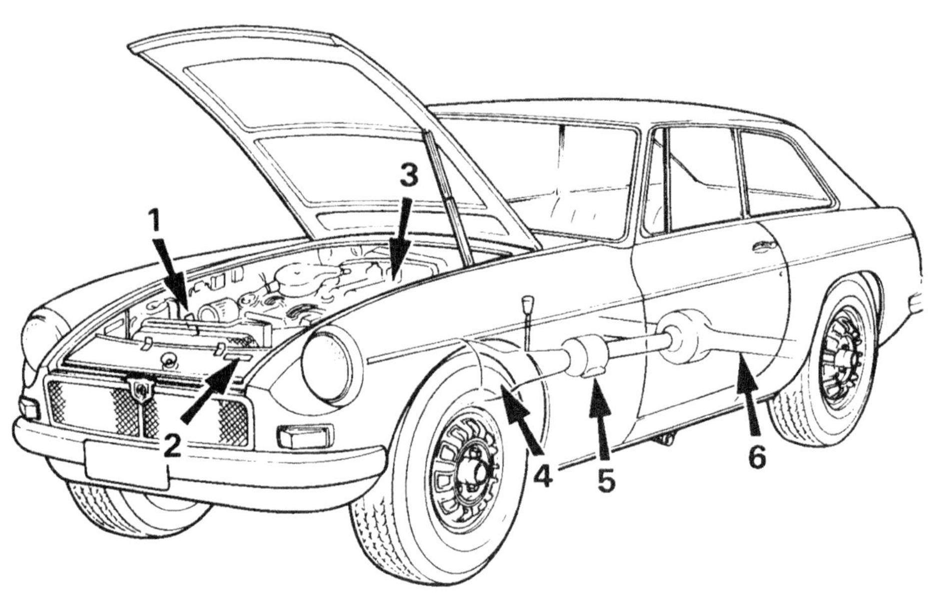

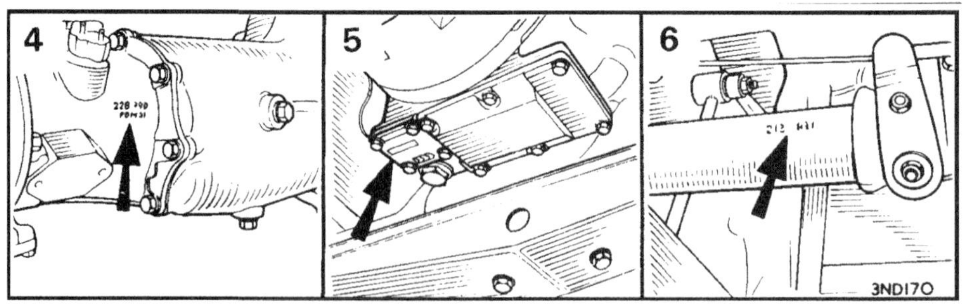

When communicating with your Distributor or Dealer always quote the car, commission and engine numbers. When the communication concerns the transmission units or body details it is necessary to quote also the transmission casing and body numbers.

(1) **Car number.** Stamped on a plate secured to the right-hand valance.

(2) **Commission number.** Stamped on a plate secured to the bonnet locking platform.

(3) **Engine number.** Stamped on the left-hand side of the cylinder block located directed behind the left-hand cylinder head.

(4) **Gearbox number.** Stamped on the right-hand side of the gearbox casing.

(5) **Overdrive unit number.** Stamped on a plate secured to the underside of the overdrive main casing.

(6) **Rear axle number.** Stamped on the left-hand side of the rear axle tube near the spring seating.

Service Parts and Accessories

Genuine **BRITISH LEYLAND** and **UNIPART** parts and accessories are designed and tested for your vehicle and have the full backing of the British Leyland Owner's Service Statement. ONLY WHEN GENUINE BRITISH LEYLAND AND UNIPART PARTS ARE USED CAN RESPONSIBILITY BE CONSIDERED UNDER THE TERMS OF THE STATEMENT.

For more information on **UNIPART,** see your British Leyland Distributor or Dealer.

Genuine British Leyland and UNIPART parts and accessories are supplied in cartons and packs bearing either or both of these symbols.

Safety features embodied in the car may be impaired if other than genuine parts are fitted. In certain territories, legislation prohibits the fitting of parts not to the vehicle manufacturer's specification. Owners purchasing accessories while travelling abroad should ensure that the accessory and its fitted location on the car conform to mandatory requirements existing in their country of origin.

Supplementary tool kit

A UNIPART Tool Kit is obtainable from all Distributors and Dealers. The kit, in a waterproof roll contains the following tools:—

8 combination spanners	2 screwdrivers
1 adjustable spanner	1 feeler gauge set
2 pairs pliers	

This kit can be supplemented from a comprehensive range of UNIPART quality hand tools which are also available.

UNIPART car care

Use of the following products selected from the UNIPART range will ensure maximum effectiveness in maintaining the appearance and condition of your vehicle.

Engine grime and grease	UNIPART Engine Cleaner
Carpets Seat and trim } .. .. Headlining	UNIPART Upholstery Cleaner
Washing	UNIPART Car Shampoo UNIPART Car Sponges UNIPART Chamois-leather
Glass	UNIPART Glass Cleaner
Bodywork	UNIPART Hi-shine Car Polish
Chrome and bright trim	UNIPART Chrome Cleaner

Winter aids:

Iced-up windscreen and windows ..	UNIPART De-Icer Spray
Washer reservoir	UNIPART 'Four Seasons' Screen Wash

Service Exchange Scheme

The Service Exchange Scheme has been designed as a money-saver.

Your Distributor or Dealer will supply any exchange unit offered for your vehicle at a price which allows for the return of the old one to us for rebuilding to 'as new' standard, at one of our specialist factories or by the original supplier. The use of this technique reduces the cost but not the quality.

Ask your Distributor or Dealer for full details and for examples of the money you can save by taking advantage of the scheme.

CLEANING

Interior *Carpets:* Clean with a semi-stiff brush or a vacuum cleaner, preferably before washing the outside of the car. Occasionally give the carpets a thorough cleaning: dilute one part **UNIPART Upholstery Cleaner** with eight parts warm water, apply vigorously with a semi-stiff brush and wipe over with a damp sponge or cloth. Carpets must not be 'dry-cleaned'.

Plastic faced upholstery: Clean with diluted **UNIPART Upholstery Cleaner.** Spot clean with **UNIPART Upholstery Cleaner** spread thinly over the surface with a brush or cloth, leave for five minutes, then wipe over with a damp sponge or cloth.

Nylon faced upholstery: Remove loose dirt with a brush or vacuum cleaner. The nylon pile has been chemically treated to resist soiling and care must be taken when cleaning. Use **UNIPART Nylon Cleaner.** To remove a stain, apply the cleaner, then pat and wipe with a clean cloth in the direction of the pile until the stain is removed. **DO NOT RUB.** When dry, gently brush against the pile, then with the pile.

UNIPART Upholstery Cleaner can be used for cleaning and renovating all the usual upholstery materials, and rubber, but it should not be used on painted surfaces.

Body Regular care of the body finish is necessary if the new appearance of the car exterior is to be maintained against the effects of air pollution, rain, and mud.

Wash the bodywork frequently, using a soft sponge and plenty of water containing **UNIPART Car Shampoo.** Large deposits of mud must be softened with water before using the sponge. Smears should be removed by a second wash in clean water, and with a sponge if necessary. When dry, clean the surface of the car with a damp chamois-leather. In addition to the regular maintenance, special attention is required if the car is driven in extreme conditions such as sea spray or on salted roads. In these conditions and with other forms of severe contamination an additional washing operation is necessary which should include underbody hosing. Any damaged areas should be immediately covered with paint and a complete repair effected as soon as possible. Before touching in light scratches and abrasions with paint, thoroughly clean the surface. Use petrol/white spirit (gasoline/hydrocarbon solvent) to remove spots of grease or tar.

The application of **UNIPART Hi-shine Car Polish** is all that is required to remove traffic film and to ensure the retention of the new appearance.

Bright trim Never use an abrasive on stainless, chromium, aluminium, or plastic bright parts and on no account clean them with metal polish. Remove spots of grease or tar with petrol/white spirit (gasoline/hydrocarbon solvent) and wash frequently with water containing **UNIPART Car Shampoo.** When the dirt has been removed polish with a clean dry cloth or chamois-leather until bright. Any slight tarnish found on stainless or plated components which have not received regular attention may be removed with **UNIPART Chrome Cleaner.** An occasional application of light mineral oil or grease will help to preserve the finish, particularly during winter when salt may be used on the roads, but these protectives must not be applied to plastic finishes.

Windscreen If windscreen smearing has occurred it can be removed with **UNIPART Glass Cleaner.**

Always keep the windscreen washer bottle topped up and add **UNIPART Screenwash** in the recommended proportions to improve visibility in adverse weather conditions. In freezing conditions use **UNIPART 'Four Seasons' Screen Wash.** Do not use radiator anti-freeze.

UNIPART products mentioned above are obtainable from your Distributor or Dealer.

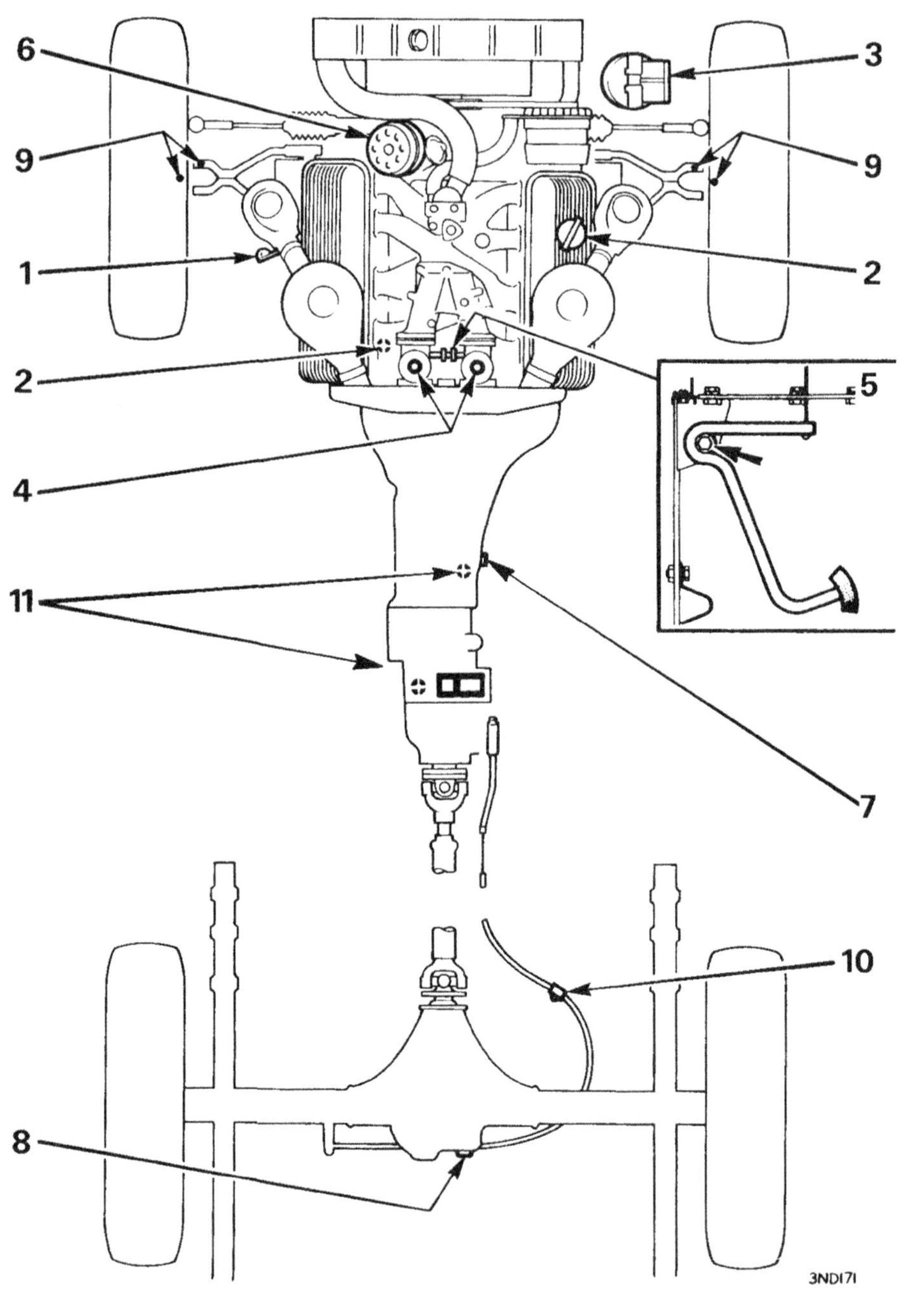
6
3
9
9
1
2
2
4
5
11
7
8
10
3ND171

NOTE.–Ensure that the vehicle is standing on a level surface when checking the oil levels.

Weekly and before a long journey
(1) ENGINE. Check the oil level with the dipstick and top up if necessary.

Every 6,000 miles (10000 km.) or 6 months
(2) ENGINE. Drain the oil and refill with new oil.

(3) ENGINE OIL FILTER. Remove the disposable filter cartridge and fit a new oil filter cartridge.

(4) CARBURETTERS. Top up the carburetter piston dampers–refer to page 58.

(5) ACCELERATOR. Lubricate accelerator control linkage, cable and pedal pivot.

(6) DISTRIBUTOR. Lubricate all parts as necessary–the cam and its felt pad, contact pivot, centrifugal weights and the centre spindle felt pad.

(7) GEARBOX AND OVERDRIVE. Check the oil level and top up if necessary.

(8) REAR AXLE. Check the oil level and top up if necessary.

(9) FRONT SUSPENSION (4 nipples)

(10) HANDBRAKE CABLE (1 nipple)

Give three or four strokes with a grease gun

LOCKS AND HINGES. Lubricate the bonnet release and safety catch, and all locks and hinges. Do not oil the steering lock.

Every 24,000 miles (40000 km.) or 24 months
(11) GEARBOX AND OVERDRIVE. Drain the oil, clean the overdrive filters and refill with new oil–refer to page 62.

Optional lubrication every 3,000 miles (5000 km.) or 3 months
(1) ENGINE. Check the oil level with the dipstick and top up if necessary.

RECOMMENDED LUBRICANTS

Component	Engine and Carburetter			Gearbox		Rear Axle and Steering Gear		Grease Points	Upper Cylinder Lubrication
Climatic conditions	All temperatures above −10°C (15°F)	Temperatures 10° to −20°C (50° to −5°F)	All temperatures below −10°C (15°F)	All temperatures above −10°C (15°F)	All temperatures below −10°C (15°F)	All temperatures above −10°C (15°F)	All temperatures below −10°C (15°F)	All conditions	All conditions
Minimum performance level	British Leyland Service Fill Lubricating Oil Specification for Passenger Car and Light Commercial Petrol Engines B.L.S. OL.02.			MIL-L-2105	MIL-L-2105	MIL-L-2105B	MIL-L-2105B	Multipurpose Lithium Grease N.L.G.I. Consistency No. 2	Upper Cylinder Lubricant
ESSO	Esso Uniflo 20W/50	Esso Uniflo 10W/30	Esso Extra Motor Oil 5W/20	Esso Gear Oil GX 90/140	Esso Gear Oil GX 80	U.K.: Gear Oil GX 90/140 Overseas: Gear Oil GX 90	Esso Gear Oil GX 80	Esso Multipurpose Grease H	Esso Upper Cylinder Lubricant
MOBIL	Mobiloil Special 20W/50 or Super 10W/50	Mobiloil Super 10W/50	Mobiloil 5W/20	Mobilube GX 90	Mobilube GX 80	Mobilube H.D. 90	Mobilube H.D. 80	Mobilgrease M.P. or M.S.	Upper Mobilube
BP	BP Super Visco-Static 20/50 or 10W/40	BP Super Visco-Static 10W/30 or 10W/40	BP Super Visco-Static or BP Super Visco-Static 5W/20	BP Gear Oil S.A.E. 90 EP	BP Gear Oil S.A.E. 80 EP	BP Hypogear 90 E.P.	BP Hypogear 80 EP	BP Energrease L 2	BP Upper Cylinder Lubricant
SHELL	Shell Super 20W/50	Shell Super 10W/50	Shell Super 5W/30	Shell Spirax 90 EP	Shell Spirax 80 EP	Shell Spirax Heavy Duty 90	Shell Spirax Heavy Duty 80	Shell Retinax A	Shell Upper Cylinder Lubricant
TEXACO	Havoline 20W/50 or 10W/40	Havoline 10W/40	Havoline 5W/30			Multigear Lubricant EP 90	Multigear Lubricant EP 80	Marfak All Purpose	Special Upper Cylinder Lubricant
PETROFINA	Fina Supergrade 20W/50 or 10W/50 or 10W/40	Fina Supergrade 10W/50 or 10W/40	Fina Supergrade 5W/20			Fina Pentonic XP 90-140	Fina Pentonic MP 80	Fina HLT 2	Fina Cyltonic
DUCKHAMS	Duckhams Motor Oil	Duckhams Q.5500	Duckhams Q.5-30	Duckhams Hypoid 90	Duckhams Hypoid 80	Duckhams Hypoid 90S	Duckhams Hypoid 80S	Duckhams L.B. 10 Grease	Duckhams Adcoid Liquid
CASTROL	Castrol GTX	Castrolite	Castrol CRI 5W/20	Castrol Hypoy	Castrol Hypoy Light	Castrol Hypoy B.90	Castrol Hypoy B.80	Castrol L.M. Grease	Castrollo

The lubrication systems of your new car are filled with high quality oils. You should always use a high quality oil of the correct viscosity range in the engine, gearbox and rear axle during subsequent maintenance operations or when topping up. The use of oils not to the recommended specification can lead to high oil and fuel consumption and, ultimately, damage to the engine, gearbox or rear axle components.

Oils to the recommended specification contain additives which disperse the corrosive acids formed by combustion and also prevent the formation of sludge which can block oilways. **Additional oil additives should not be used.** Servicing intervals must be adhered to.

Engine Use a well-known brand of oil to B.L.S. O.L. O.R. or MIL-L-2104B or A.P.I. SE quality, with a viscosity band spanning the temperature range of your locality.

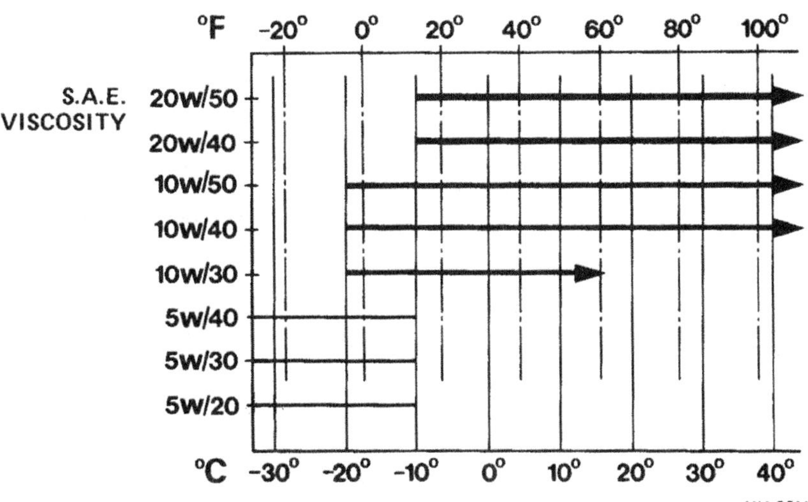

Synchromesh gearbox Top up and refill with EP 90 (MIL-L-2105) above −10°C (15°F) or EP 80 (MIL-L-2105) below −10°C (15°F).

Rear axle and steering rack Top up and refill with HD 90 (MIL-L-2105B) above −10°C (15°F) or HD 80 (MIL-L-2105B) below −10°C (15°F).

Grease points Use Multipurpose Lithium Grease N.L.G.I. consistency No. 2.

BATTERY
Access
Fig. 1

Release the rear seat cushion securing straps from the fasteners, and pull the cushion forward.

Remove the carpet covering the rear compartment floor. Turn the three quick-release fasteners (1) anti-clockwise one half turn and remove the battery compartment cover panel. (2).

Checking
topping-up
Fig. 1

The vehicle must be on level ground when the electrolyte is being checked.

DO NOT USE A NAKED LIGHT WHEN CHECKING THE LEVELS and do not use tap water for topping-up.

Remove the battery vent cover vertically by using the grip at the centre of the cover (3); this will ensure that the filling valves are operated correctly. If no electrolyte is visible inside the battery, pour distilled or deionised water into the filling trough (4) until the six tubes (5) and the connecting trough (6) are filled. Refit the vent cover.

The above operations should not be carried out within half an hour of the battery having been charged, other than by the vehicle's own generating system. In extremely cold conditions run the engine immediately after topping-up so as to mix the electrolyte.

IMPORTANT: The vent cover must be kept closed at all times, except when topping-up. The electrolyte will flood if the cover is removed for long periods during or within thirty minutes of the battery being normal (6.5 amp) charged. Single-cell discharge testers cannot be used on these batteries. Operation of the filling device will be destroyed if the battery case is drilled or punctured.

General
maintenance

The batteries must be kept dry and clean; cable and battery terminals should be smeared with petroleum jelly.

Do not leave the battery in a discharged state for any length of time. When not in regular use have the battery fully charged, and every four weeks give a short refresher trickle charge to prevent permanent damage to the battery plates.

Fig. 1

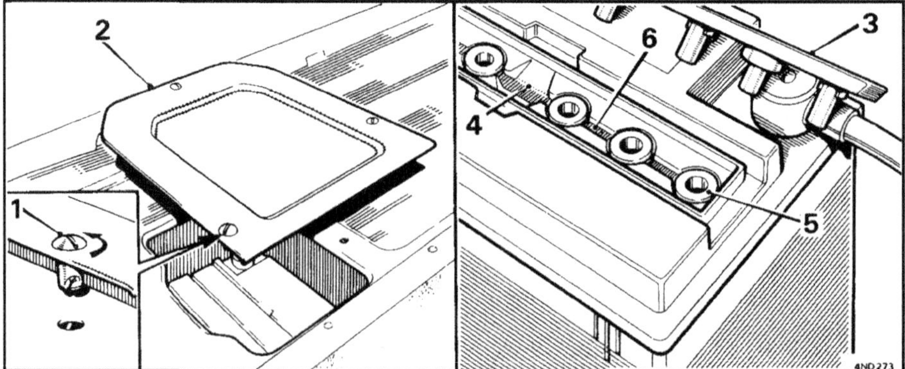

Removing Ease the bottom of the outer rim (1) forwards away from the lamp. Unscrew the three inner rim retaining screws (2), remove the inner rim (3), withdraw the light unit (4), and disconnect the three-pin plug (5).

Refitting. Connect the three-pin plug and position the light unit in the headlamp body ensuring that the three lugs formed on the outer edge of the light unit engage in the slots formed in the body, and fit the inner retaining rim. Position the outer rim on the retaining lugs, press the rim downwards and inwards.

Beam setting
Fig. 2

Two adjusting screw are provided on each headlamp for setting the main beams. The screw (6) is for adjusting the beam in the vertical plane, and the screw (7) is for horizontal adjustment. The beams must be set in accordance with local regulations. Resetting and checking should be entrusted to your Distributor or Dealer, who will have special equipment available for this purpose.

Fig. 2

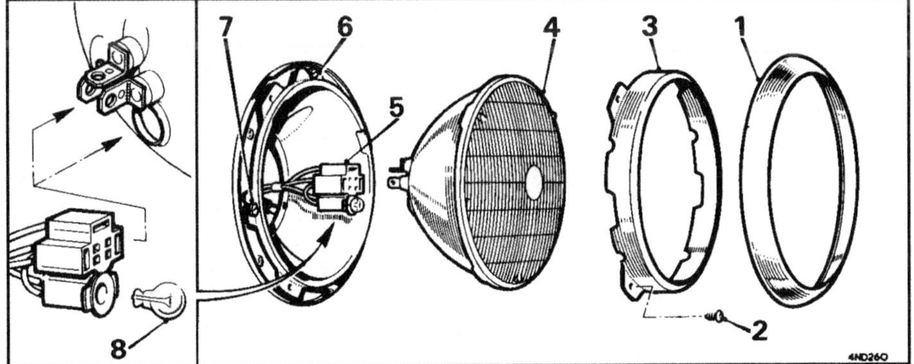

LAMPS
Pilot
Fig. 2

The pilot lamp bulbs are incorporated in the headlamps. To gain access to the bulb, remove the sealed beam light unit (4) and disconnect the three-pin socket and bulb holder (5); the capless-type bulb can then be withdrawn.

Direction
indicator
Fig.3

To gain access to the parking and direction indicator bulb (1), unscrew the two retaining screws (2) and withdraw the rim and lens.

Number-plate
Fig. 4

Slacken the screw (1), remove the metal cover (2) and glass lens (3). Press in and turn the required bulb to release it from the bulb holder. When refitting, ensure the glass lens engages over the raised portion at each side of the seal and that the sealing washer is fitted to the cover retaining screw.

		Volts	*Watts*	*Part No.*
Replacement	Pilot lamp (capless-type bulb)	12	5	GLB 501
bulbs	Number-plate lamp	12	6	GLB 989

Fig. 3

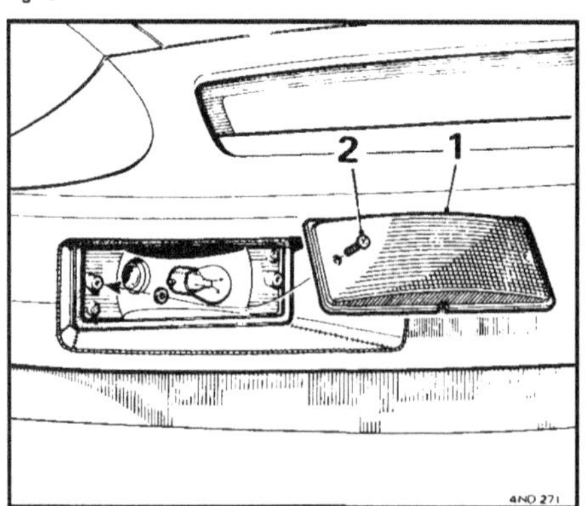

Fig. 4

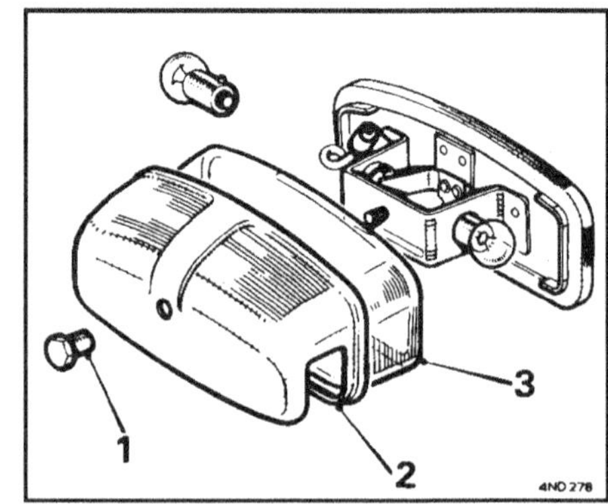

GENERAL DATA

Gearbox Overall ratio: First .. .. .. 9.33 : 1 (from Gearbox No. 103144)

Dimensions
- Length .. .. 13 ft. 2¼ in. (4.02 m.)
- Width .. .. 4 ft. 11 5/16 in. (152.3 cm.)
- Height .. .. 4 ft. 2 7/8 in. (129.2 cm.)
- Ground clearance (minimum) .. 3¼ in. (82.55 mm.)
- Track: Front .. .. 4 ft. 1 in. (124.4 cm.)
- Rear .. .. 4 ft. 1¼ in. (125.0 cm.)
- Wheelbase .. .. 7 ft. 7 in. (231.1 cm.)
- Turning circle .. .. .. 32 ft. (9.75 m.)
- Toe-in .. .. 1/16 to 3/32 in. (1.6 to 2.4 mm.)

Weights

Loading condition		Total weight	Distribution	
			Front	Rear
Kerbside	Including full fuel tank and all optional extras	2529 lb. (1148 kg.)	1268 lb. (575 kg.)	1261 lb. (571 kg.)
Normal	Kerbside weight including driver and passenger	2829 lb. (1284 kg.)	1383 lb. (627 kg.)	1446 lb. (655 kg.)
Gross	Maximum weight condition— refer to note below	2979 lb. (1352 kg.)	1338 lb. (606 kg.)	1641 lb. (744 kg.)
Maximum permissible towing weight		1680 lb. (762 kg.)		
Maximum towbar hitch load		100 lb. (45 kg.)		
Maximum roof rack load		50 lb. (23 kg.)		

NOTE: Due consideration must be given to the overall weight carried when fully loading the car. Any load carried on the roof rack or downward load from a towing hitch must also be included in the gross car weight.

ISBN 9781869826710   Part No. AKD 8423 (4th Edition)   10W4/2147   Ref: MG78HH

OFFICIAL TECHNICAL BOOKS

Brooklands Technical Books has been formed to supply owners, restorers and professional repairers with official factory literature.

Workshop Manuals

Midget Instruction Manual		9781855200739
Midget TD & TF	AKD580A	9781870642552
MGA 1500 1600 & 1600 Mk. 2	AKD600D	9781869826307
MGA Twin Cam	AKD926B	9781855208179
Austin-Healey Sprite Mk. 2, Mk. 3 & Mk. 4 and MG Midget Mk. 1, Mk. 2 & Mk. 3	AKD4021	9781855202818
Midget 1500	AKM4071B	9781855201699
MGB & MGB GT	AKD3259 & AKD4957	9781855201743
MGB GT V8 Supplement		9781855201859
MGB, MGB GT and MGB GT V8		9781783180578
MGC	AKD 7133	9781855201828
Rover 25 & MG ZR 1999-2005	RCL0534ENGBB	9781855208834
Rover 75 & MG ZT 1999-2005	RCL0536ENGBB	9781855208841
MGF - 1.6 MPi, 1.8 MPi, 1.8VVC RCL 0051ENG, RCL0057ENG & RCL0124		9781855207165
MGF Electrical Manual 1996-2000 MY	RCL0341	9781855209077
MG TF	RCL0493	9781855207493

Parts Catalogues

MGA 1500	AKD1055	9781870642569
MGA 1600 Mk. 1 & Mk. 2	AKD1215	9781870642613
Austin-Healey Sprite Mk. 1 & Mk. 2 and MG Midget Mk. 1 (Mechanical & Body Edition)	AKD3566 & AKD3567	9781783180509
Austin-Healey Sprite Mk. 3 & Mk. 4 and MG Midget Mk. 2 & Mk. 3 (Mechanical & Body Edition 1969)	AKD3513 & AKD3514	9781783180554
Austin-Healey Sprite Mk. 3 & Mk. 4 and MG Midget Mk. 2 & Mk. 3 (Feb 1977 Edition)	AKM0036	9780948207419
MGB up to Sept 1976	AKM0039	9780948207068
MGB Sept 1976 on	AKM0037	9780948207440

Owners Handbooks

Midget Series TD		9781870642910
Midget TF and TF 1500 Operation Manual	AKD658A	9781870642934
MGA 1500	AKD598G	9781855202924
MGA 1600	AKD1172C	9781855201668
MGA 1600 Mk. 2	AKD1958A	9781855201675
MGA Twin Cam (Operation)	AKD879	9781855207929
MGA Twin Cam (Operation)	AKD879B	9781855207936
MGA 1500 Special Tuning	AKD819A	9781783181728
MGA 1500 and 1600 Mk. 1 Special Tuning	AKD819B	9781783181735
Midget TF and TF 1500	AKD210A	9781855202979
Midget Mk. 3 (GB 1967-74)	AKD7596	9781855201477
Midget (Pub 1978)	AKM3229	9781855200906
Midget Mk. 3 (US 1967-74)	AKD7883	9781855206311
Midget Mk. 3 (US 1976)	AKM3436	9781855201767
Midget Mk. 3 (US 1979)	AKM4386	9781855201774
MGB Tourer (Pub 1965)	AKD3900C	9781869826741

MGB Tourer & GT (Pub 1969)	AKD3900J	9781855200609
MGB Tourer & GT (Pub 1974)	AKD7598	9781869826727
MGB Tourer & GT (Pub 1976)	AKM3661	9781869826703
MGB GT V8	AKD8423	9781869826710
MGB Tourer & GT (US 1968)	AKD7059B	9781870642514
MGB Tourer & GT (US 1971)	AKD7881	9781870642521
MGB Tourer & GT (US 1973)	AKD8155	9781870642538
MGB Tourer (US 1975)	AKD3286	9781870642545
MGB (US 1979)	AKM8098	9781855200722
MGB Tourer & GT Tuning	CAKD4034L	9780948207051
MGB Special Tuning 1800cc	AKD4034	9780948207006
MGC	AKD4887B	9781869826734
MGF (Modern shape)	RCL0332ENG	9781855208339

Owners Workshop Manuals - Autobooks

MGA & MGB & GT 1955-1968 (Glove Box Autobooks Manual)	9781855200937
MGA & MGB & GT 1955-1968 (Autobooks Manual)	9781783180356
Austin-Healey Sprite Mk. 1, 2, 3 & 4 and MG Midget Mk. 1, 2, 3 & 1500 1958-1980 (Glove Box Autobooks Manual)	9781855201255
Austin-Healey Sprite Mk. 1, 2, 3 & 4 and MG Midget Mk. 1, 2, 3 & 1500 1958-1980 (Autobooks Manual)	9781783180332
MGB & MGB GT 1968-1981 (Glove Box Autobooks Manual)	9781855200944
MGB & MGB GT 1968-1981 (Autobooks Manual)	9781783180325

Carburetters

SU Carburetters Tuning Tips & Techniques	9781855202559
Solex Carburetters Tuning Tips & Techniques	9781855209770
Weber Carburettors Tuning Tips and Techniques	9781855207592

Restoration Guide

MG T Series Restoration Guide	9781855202115
MGA Restoration Guide	9781855203020
Restoring Sprites & Midgets	9781855205987
Practical Classics On MGB Restoration	9780946489428

MG - Road Test Books

MG Gold Portfolio 1929-1939	9781855201941
MG TA & TC GOLD PORT 1936-1949	9781855203150
MG TD & TF Gold Portfolio 1949-1955	9781855203167
MG Y-Type & Magnette Road Test Portfolio	9781855208629
MGB & MGC GT V8 GP 1962-1980	9781855200715
MGA & Twin Cam Gold Portfolio 1955-1962	9781855200784
MGB Roadsters 1962-1980	9781869826109
MGC & MGB GT V8 LEX	9781855203631
MG Midget Road Test Portfolio 1961-1979	9781855208957
MGF & TF Performance Portfolio 1995-2005	9781855207073
Road & Track On MG Cars 1949-1961	9780946489398
Road & Track On MG Cars 1962-1980	9780946489817

Printed in Dunstable, United Kingdom